Early Childhood Programs

Early Childhood Programs

ORGANIZATION AND ADMINISTRATION

Cathy S. Jording, Ed.S.

ELEMENTARY SCHOOL PRINCIPAL (KY)

Michael Richardson, Ed.D.

CLEMSON UNIVERSITY

Jackson L. Flanigan, Ed.D.

CLEMSON UNIVERSITY

TECHNOMIC
PUBLISHING CO., INC.
LANCASTER · BASEL

Early Childhood Programs

a **TECHNOMIC**®publication

Published in the Western Hemisphere by
Technomic Publishing Company, Inc.
851 New Holland Avenue
Box 3535
Lancaster, Pennsylvania 17604 U.S.A.

Distributed in the Rest of the World by
Technomic Publishing AG

Printed in the United States of America
10 9 8 7 6 5 4 3 2 1

Main entry under title:
  Early Childhood Programs: Organization and Administration

A Technomic Publishing Company book·
Bibliography: p.
Includes index p. 229

Library of Congress Card No. 92-60849
ISBN No. 0-87762-881-5

CONTENTS

NINE: HEALTH AND SAFETY   161

TEN: SCHOOL-COMMUNITY RELATIONS   169

A CHILD IS NOT A VESSEL TO BE FILLED
BUT A FLAME TO BE LIGHTED.
                              —Henry Steele Commager

AS preschool and day-care programs become mandatory throughout our society, we as educators find ourselves faced with the monumental question, "How do we establish excellent programs on shoestring budgets?"

In preparing this guide, we have formulated ideas, forms, procedures, and varied information that we have used during the past several years. We have also included some of the pitfalls we experienced, in the hope that awareness of these will make the reader better prepared to deal with them. The intent of the guide is to make starting and administering an early childhood program as simple as possible.

Having the opportunity to read about an actual working program may help to begin a program more efficiently. Programs will only be as good as hard work and perseverance allow.

This management guide is written to explain the establishment and operation of a preschool program. The material contained may be used to develop a preschool program in any environment, public or private. Forms, letters, regulations, procedures, and other pertinent information used within the guide are adaptable to most situations. Regulations will differ by state. Always check with the appropriate state agencies for exact regulations that apply to individual programs.

The guide is divided into two large sections—Preschool Programs and Day-Care Programs—and is arranged in a manner that permits the reader to find specific material easily. Some areas will overlap and thus will be found or referenced in more than one section of the book.

The chapters are divided into areas of concern: program survey, development, purpose, regulations, administration, financing, enrollment, curriculum, and day-care. Within each area, various methods of implementation are discussed. Curriculum is discussed, with emphasis given to programs that are appropriate in terms of both age and development for the early childhood area. Day-care materials are discussed in detail in the final chapter.

The entire book is based on experience, and was developed from working programs that have been used and tested. The material in the following pages has been an integral part of an existing program consisting of 250–300 students per year and fifteen to eighteen staff members.

The authors hope the experiences within this manual will prove valuable both to the professional and to the novice in developing and implementing high-quality early childhood programs. As the needs of young children expand, this manual can assist those who dedicate their lives to meeting those needs.

For directors, the material will provide a guide to developing an active program from idea to reality. For the teacher the chapters concerning facility, enrollment, curriculum, health and safety, and parents will assist in preparing and maintaining a high-quality development-based program. The information concerning the utilization of parents as partners will also be of particular interest. For the university student, the book will provide an understanding of how an effective program is developed and maintained. Students will see that effective programs do not just happen—they evolve through the labor of dedicated people.

Chapter One provides information on program planning and feasibility. The material is designed to assist in pre-planning and critical analysis processes, including assessing the need of the community, determining the type of program to be developed, writing the purpose statement, and complying with state regulations. This chapter will assist planners in deciding whether the program will be economically feasible according to the community need.

Chapter Two outlines the inner core of the program. Discussed is the development of a responsible Board of Directors, and the creation of long- and short-term goals. A school policy must be created with consideration given to all areas of concern, and this chapter provides suggestions for items that should be included.

Chapter Three covers the central element of the working program—the administrator. The material includes a detailed discussion of the qualifications and background of an effective early childhood program director. The material outlines specific responsibilities of the director, spanning all areas of the program. Supervision of the director by the board, while keeping in mind the responsibilities of board members as monitors of the program, is discussed.

As with all business ventures, financing is a major part of a program. Chapter Four provides a detailed examination of all areas of financing. The material discusses funding, types of income, cost analysis, budgeting, and planning. The management section includes information on salary schedules, staff financial records, taxes, financial reports, and bookkeeping materials. The chapter concludes with a discussion of the use of computers and realistic monetary sources, together with suggestions that will make an early childhood education program one of quality, even if running on a shoestring budget.

Every program utilizes a facility. Chapter Five discusses preparation of the building and grounds for an early childhood education program. Indoor and outdoor space requirements, along with calculations, inspections, and the equipment necessary to provide a developmentally appropriate program, are included in this chapter. The section on classrooms gives a total listing of what is appropriate for the young child. Interest centers and systems for management help make the classroom enjoyable for the child. Types and sizes of equipment and materials are included for interest centers, with a diagram of a room arrangement, materials in storage areas, teacher workroom, and director's office. This chapter focuses on the facility and how to utilize it to the fullest.

Chapter Six covers enrollment, from recruitment to release. Types of recruitment are given with examples of advertisements. Registration methods and procedures are outlined, including types of parent correspondence, application samples, tuition for multiple children, and permission forms. Ideas for child identification, staff orientation, and parent-child orientation are also presented. This chapter covers every aspect of placing and maintaining the child in the program, and provides examples of materials that have been field-tested.

In Chapter Seven, "Curriculum," an overview of the four curriculum areas of early childhood education is provided. The discussion of the four areas is provided as a guide for further reading and understanding of early childhood education and its role in each preschool program. For convenience, a detailed list of both equipment and activities has been included to help make development of the program simpler. The activities are listed by specific curriculum areas. The planning section has examples and definitions of types of teacher planning, child skills, and child and parent evaluation. At the end of the chapter is a suggested reading list, which will help further the educator's knowledge of what is appropriate to teach the young child.

Staff will be a determining factor for the success of each program. In Chapter Eight, guidelines for selection of staff are foremost. The chapter discusses qualifications and responsibilities of both teachers and assistants. Employment is discussed and the following items are covered: recruitment, laws governing selection, and advertising. Discussion of interviewing techniques and the "do's and don'ts" of inquiry are listed. Also included is information that needs to be included in each staff member's file. Orientation, in-service, evaluation, observation, contracts, and records are also discussed. In the final pages of the chapter a section is devoted to the release of a staff member and procedures to be followed. There are examples of staff records throughout the chapter to assist in preparing a program.

Since all children have special needs and must be provided a safe atmosphere, Chapter Nine discusses areas of health and safety. The first section of the chapter deals with developmental delays and how to handle these special children. Because accidents and disease often happen, a section is included on reporting and policy concerning both areas. Material concerning child abuse, including a listing of indicators, is also presented. In the section on safety, information is provided concerning the creation of a safe environment, disaster plans, drills, and safety rules. Because a safe and healthy environment is of top priority, this chapter gives basic information for creating a safe and orderly place for young children.

Chapter Ten covers every aspect of using parents and community resources. A detailed discussion concerning relating to and working with parents is presented in the first section. The remainder of the material outlines the use of volunteers and evaluations of the program, and closes with a section of "How to Use Your Local Resources." This chapter will assist in making the community and its wealth a part of an early childhood education program.

The Final Chapter discusses day-care, its purposes, and development. Since day-care is an extension of a preschool day, planning, curriculum, and most areas of programming are similar. Pre-planning, because of stricter state regulations, is looked at in more detail. This chapter gives greater emphasis to areas of early childhood that are strictly under day-care. This chapter goes through the steps needed to implement and monitor a day-care program and offers numerous examples, forms, and letters. Included is a section on closing a program with the least trauma to all involved. Day-care programs are in demand, but not as "baby-sitting" programs. This chapter assists in developing a high-quality, developmentally planned program.

The intent of this book is to serve as a guide and a resource in daily planning. Even if the content does not fit exactly into a program, the provided forms and suggestions will give many helpful ideas that can be easily modified and implemented. Early childhood education has a major impact on the way our children learn in later years. Early childhood educators have the responsibility to make these programs the best possible, so that our children will have a bright future.

ACKNOWLEDGEMENTS

THIS Preschool Management Guide is the product of numerous years of experience as a preschool director, an early childhood consultant, and an early childhood education instructor.

A special thank you to all who have supported our efforts, particularly our families.

To Marvis, Leah, and Roslyn.

CHAPTER ONE

In the Beginning

...COME, MY FRIENDS,
'TIS NOT TOO LATE TO SEEK A NEWER WORLD.
—Alfred Lord Tennyson

"IN the Beginning"—how often have we heard those words, and felt our thoughts overwhelming us? Used here, the words mean "to create." In creating an early childhood education program, either preschool or day-care, we first must ask ourselves—"Why?" If the program is being developed to produce added income immediately, the goal may not be realistic. An early childhood education program will not add income. If anything, it will strain your finances for the first few years before the program becomes self-supporting.

Secondly, if a church-related early childhood program has as a function and purpose the desire to gain members, it is very possible that new families will not be received into church membership for several years. Remember, these programs are sowing the seeds of faith. Those seeds must be cultivated carefully, and if the church reaps the harvest of that planting within five years, the program has been successful.

Do not begin an early childhood program expecting to reap the benefits immediately. Begin the program as an outreach—welcoming *all* children and teaching the wondrous gift of love. Amazingly, one day these children, with whom you have shared, may return when they are looking for a church home.

The love and training received from the program will be remembered for many years after the children have left. As can be expected, this process does not happen quickly, so be patient and practice perseverance. Ask yourself, "What is my purpose for developing an early childhood education program?" The development of such a purpose for the program should be the first decision made by the investors. A sample statement is shown in Figure 1.

ABC Preschool is a nonprofit organization whose purpose is to provide a consistently superior educational experience in a humanistic setting. The program provides each child with socialization, creative play, art, music, story time, physical activities, and educational learning experiences in accordance with the individual child's age and ability. The programs are further designed to help the child develop habits of observation and expression. The child learns to make free choices, so long as he/she stays within the limits of consideration for people and things. The child is not expected to conform to an arbitrarily imposed norm of behavior.

The child is continually challenged, in subtle ways, to achieve specific learning goals enabling him/her to gain increasing meaning from the surrounding environment; to develop an awareness of concepts; to interpret sensory experiences; and ultimately to take the prerequisite steps for developing his/her mind in preparation to begin to read and perform other academic tasks.

The programs are designed to give each child time to grow (mentally and emotionally) to explore, to experiment, to discover, to play, to love, and above all, time to be a child.

Figure 1. Example of a purpose statement.

Type of Program

The purpose statement should be developed to meet an individual purpose. Make sure this purpose is consistent with program objectives. After establishing the purpose, identify the type of program that is needed because there is a great deal of difference between a preschool and a day-care program.

DAY-CARE

A day-care program is typically an all-day program, usually from 6:30 A.M. to 5:30 P.M. It is intended for children of working parents. A child will usually be in this type of program for nine hours per day, five days per week, and forty-eight to fifty weeks during the year. The program must be well-planned and scheduled, so as not to become monotonous to the child and staff. The program should not be merely a baby-sitting service. The use of television should be limited to educational programs, if it is to be used at all. There should be growth and educational programs during all hours of operation, and activities should be planned for the entire time a child is present. (Refer to the chapter on day-care for more detailed information.)

Extra equipment will be needed for preparing and serving meals, and cots will be needed for napping. Staff will need to be employed according to the number of children. (Staff-child ratios are determined by your state agency regulations.) Initially a day-care center requires added expense for equipment, materials, and backup financial aid for the program. This type of program can be expensive until it proves self-supporting, which may take three to five years. Because of the expense, an entrepreneur should weigh the pros and cons very carefully before beginning a day-care program. Be realistic in estimating both initial start-up and maintenance costs—a shoestring budget will not be realistic for this type of program.

PRESCHOOL

The preschool second program is called by various names, such as *playschool, nursery school,* or *preschool.* For the sake of discussion, the term *preschool* or *early childhood education* is used throughout the book to describe this type of program. There are many variations of the preschool program schedules—two days per week, three days per week, four days per week, five days per week, Mother's Day Out (one day per week), and many other variations. This program is usually half a day in length, lasting from two to three hours. It can run only in the morning, or only in the afternoon, or can be expanded to have both morning and afternoon sessions.

The programs are educational in nature, with emphasis on preparation for entrance to kindergarten or first grade. Licensing falls under the jurisdiction of the individual state department of education, and must meet its criteria for operation. Preschool is typically a nine to ten month program, with no school or just a short session during the summer. Financing this sort of program is simpler, with minimal start-up costs and operating costs coming from tuition and fees. Preschools can be self-supporting within a shorter period of time, and will not drain finances as readily. For a small operation, this program is more feasible.

Both day-care and preschools are needed in today's society. In order to determine which is right for the community, conduct a survey of the surrounding area to determine the need. Figure 2 is an example of a minimal survey instrument.

Community Need Survey

This community need survey can be mailed, distributed door to door, distributed to churches, or published in newspapers. Survey information can also be taken by telephone. After tabulating the survey, the need is determined, including financial considerations and facility preparation based on what program will best suit the circumstances. Do not become unduly skeptical if the decision does not totally match the need.

(school letterhead)

_____ is conducting this survey to ascertain the feasibility of starting one of the following programs. Please fill out the information below, stating which program would best serve your needs, and return it to the above address. Thank you!!

_____ Day-Care (6:30 A.M.–6:30 P.M.)

_____ Half-Day Preschool Program

Would you participate in the program marked? __ yes __ no

Name: _____

Address: _____

Phone number: _____

Children's ages: _____
  (who would attend)

Figure 2. Community need survey.

Surveying reaches only a small portion of the community. Remember, continued advertisement will further the pool of applicants. Implement the program that fits within the allotted financial budget. The most important consideration is to give the program more than one year to evaluate its success or failure. Word of mouth is the best advertisement and will feed the program in the future.

Preliminary Contacts

Contact the state fire marshall for inspection of the facility. Explain the intent and the type of program to be started. Carry a notebook during the inspection and write down the changes or modifications that need to be made to start the program. Determine the costs of repairs or remodeling to meet specifications, and include these in start-up cost estimates. Make sure to determine differences in regulations between the two types of programs. Day-care regulations are usually more rigid, so it is best to know both for future reference.

Also, the state and/or health department must check the facility to assure compliance with their regulations. Again, if alterations are necessary, estimate the cost before final budget preparation is completed.

Each of these programs and their specific regulations and preparations will be discussed in detail within specific sections of this book.

CHAPTER TWO

Getting Started

DARING IDEAS ARE LIKE CHESSMEN MOVED FORWARD.
THEY MAY BE BEATEN, BUT THEY MAY START
A WINNING GAME.

—Goethe

WHEN everyone is ready for the project to go, consult with an accountant and/or lawyer. Remember, there are going to be many questions that will need detailed answers. For example, money—who is going to pay for the start-up costs? Will this be a loan? What costs will be shared by the program director, owner, and investors, if any? Who is responsible if the program fails? Who will pay for repairs and maintenance? When will the program be self-supporting? Questions, questions!

The Board of Directors (Corporate Board for a Private School)

This board is the link between the school and its constituents. Its function is to coordinate and establish policy for the program. The board could include members who represent:

- the school (director)
- school staff (teacher appointed)
- financial representative (accountant)
- member-at-large (community)
- parent of school child (if possible)
- lawyer (legal advisor)

The persons can be elected or appointed depending on the advice of counsel.

The board is reponsible for the operation of all areas of the school. The board will:

- develop the purpose of the school
- develop the policies under which the school will operate

- develop the educational programs to be offered in accordance with the school's purpose
- select, work with, and evaluate the director, and develop his/her ability to employ staff
- determine and check the financial management of the school
- report regularly to the community
- provide a liaison between school, parents, children, and community
- render decisions and evaluations in a consistent manner
- employ outside consultants when it is deemed necessary
- determine future needs through goal setting and vision
- solve problems, both internally and externally, in a quick, fair, and consistent manner
- perform other such duties as required by the school or by law

The persons elected or appointed to this board should be persons of integrity, commitment, and vision, who:

- work toward the school's purpose at all times
- are advocates of the school and its children
- manage the school's mission by promoting problem solving, and working toward the purpose for which the school was formed

All boards should have a legal advisor, either on the board or on retainer. Today there are many legal complications with programs; planning ahead with legal counsel makes realization of future goals seem less threatening. The school board

---

ABC Preschool admits students of any religion, race, color, national and ethnic origin, to all the rights, privileges, programs, and activities generally accorded or made available to students of the school. It does not discriminate on the basis of religion, race, color, national and ethnic origin, in administration of its educational policies, admission policies, or other school-administered programs.

Figure 3. *Admission policy.*

Children must be at least three years old and toilet-trained before entering regular preschool classes.

A child is enrolled in a class upon receipt of a completed application form and registration fee. Children may be enrolled by phone and accepted after receiving the registration fee.

Kindergarten children must be five years old by October 1 to be enrolled, and must have a birth certificate, health examination, and immunization certificate on file at school.

Figure 4. Admission requirements, ABC Preschool.

should hold meetings at least monthly. An organizational meeting should be held annually at which time board officers are elected. Typically, a chairperson, vice-chairperson, and secretary are needed to effectively and efficiently perform board functions.

School Policy

Development of the school policy is an important part of the board's activity. This policy should include (as required by federal law) a statement of nondiscrimination as illustrated in Figure 3.

Also the school policy should specify any other requirements concerning a child's entrance into school, as shown in Figure 4.

Regulations concerning admission of handicapped children must also be included.

Goals

Planning for the future is an absolute necessity for preschool programs. Setting goals does not mandate rigidity – circumstances may require a change of direction, but setting goals for three, five, and ten years helps give the school a future direction. In setting these goals, try to "see the vision" of what the school will actually be like in the years to come. Daydream about the possibilities, and visualize the best future for the school – that is the essence of "visioning."

CHAPTER THREE

Developing and Creating

IN CREATING, THE ONLY HARD THING'S TO BEGIN;
A GRASS-BLADE'S NO EASIER TO MAKE THAN AN OAK.
—James Russell Lowell

Administration

AS with all business functions, the key to a good early childhood program is the director or administrator of the program. The person chosen to head the program must be dedicated to the school's purpose, policy, and vision. The director's focus should be on educational excellence within the program. The school's mission is to provide the best possible program for the child, and the director's function is to bring that mission to life in the day-to-day operation of the school.

Job Description

The job description for the school director will be the most important the school board will write. This person will be the foundation of the program and its future. Specific responsibilities become the guide within which the director will function, and should be addressed in the job description. There are three major areas of concern in the director's job description:

(1) Statement of the school's policy and purpose
(2) Role and qualifications
(3) Responsibilities of the director

Policy and Purpose

The director's job description contains the written policy and purpose statement of the school. This guides the director in

11

planning and implementing responsibilities, and in determining how, when, and by whom the responsibilities will be carried out. The purpose statement governs the relationship between the school board and the director. Consequently, the purpose statement is the foundation for everything included within school policy. The purposes of the school should always be included in all staff job descriptions, so that each employee will understand the central vision of the school. Some typical policies are shown in Figure 5.

A statement of policy for the handling of concerns within the staff should also be included, symbolizing the structure of authority.

Figure 6 illustrates the line of authority within the school structure. The director is accountable to the school board and should be required to attend each monthly meeting.

Qualifications

The director's qualifications are determined by the school board. The director should have a background in early childhood education. Whether this background is a college degree and/or teaching experience can be determined by the school board. (If possible a director should possess a college degree.)

The director should be an advocate of early childhood education and be a humanistic administrator. Love and concern for children should also be determining factors. Above all, the director's dedication to the purpose and policies of the school must be established. The director must be willing to share talents, to grow professionally, and to affirm his/her position openly.

The director should be:

- honest
- cheerful
- conscientious
- dependable
- knowledgeable in early childhood education
- organized
- adept at handling financial budgets and records

(1) Each teacher is responsible for her own educational curriculum as approved and reviewed by the director.

(2) Each teacher is to teach the approved curriculum once each day per class for the entire school year.

(3) Each single staff member hired will receive full salary and benefits beginning August 1.

(4) Pregnancy Leave: ABC Preschools will follow the existing policy of _____ County public schools.

(5) Staff members in either preschool or day-care will not be allowed to instruct their own children in their classrooms.

Figure 5. Typical school board policies.

- a good communicator
- reliable
- flexible
- able to love children and parents without prejudice
- trustworthy
- able to provide confidentiality
- creative
- willing to share in all duties of the school
- able to delegate authority
- able to love each child, staff member, and parent as a person

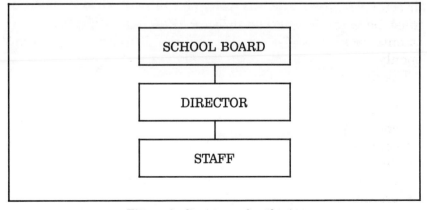

Figure 6. Structure of authority.

- an advocate
- professional at all times
- able to manage children, staff, and parents in a consistent and efficient manner
- available when needed
- responsive to criticism without malice
- able to perform all administrative and teaching functions of the school when needed

The director is the focal point of the program, and needs to be selected with extreme care and thought. The director can make or break the program. This is an extremely important job, but the director needs support from the school board, the community, and the staff. The director's position is often a thankless job requiring many hours of extra, unpaid time, whether at the school or at home. Consequently, the director is the liaison for all the school's functions. The director must be dedicated and willing to give his/her all to the program; if not, the program will most often fail.

Responsibilities of the Director

The specific responsibilities listed within the director's job description should be clear statements of the director's duties. Each responsibility should be a statement of the purpose and policy as the director is directed to implement them. The following sample statements are only guidelines. Each school should determine responsibilities that fit the school's purpose and policy. These statements can be combined to form the director's job description.

SCHOOL CLIMATE

The director is required to

- provide an educational program within the classroom
- provide leadership and guidance for staff
- provide avenues for learning for children, staff, and parents
- provide information on counseling for staff and parents
- be the liaison between the community, staff, parents, and children

- provide safe equipment for indoor and outdoor areas
- provide an environment appropriate to the age and ability of the child
- provide positive experiences between staff, parents, children, and community
- provide an orderly climate within the school

MANAGEMENT

The director is required to:

- operate within the purpose and policy of the school
- serve as an advisor to the school board
- recommend goals and policies as needed to accomplish the purpose of the school

FINANCIAL

The director is required to:

- coordinate and approve all expenditures
- keep accurate records of tuition and fees paid from each child
- file federal, state, and local taxes
- submit monthly financial reports
- assist in developing the annual budget
- keep school expenditures within the budget
- keep accurate, up-to-date financial records
- pay staff and expenditures on time
- make regular deposits
- keep accurate fund-raising records
- prepare notices from policies of board, on nonpayment of fees
- secure tax-exempt status

LIAISON

The director is required to:

- represent the school at community activities
- provide material and programs for parents and the community to promote the school's purpose

- promote good public relations between parents, school, and community
- develop a monthly newsletter
- plan parent education programs
- provide an "open-door" policy for parents
- implement parent-teacher conferences
- provide opportunities to communicate the school's purpose to the community
- coordinate all activities within the school

ENROLLMENT

The director is required to:

- secure adequate enrollment through active recruitment of students
- promote the school within the church and the community
- provide enrollment materials that reflect the school's purpose, policies, and fees
- establish class enrollments that meet state regulations
- facilitate meetings for parent and child orientation
- provide proper class size for the appropriate education of the child

ADMINISTRATION

The director is required to:

- meet all regulations as stated by the federal, state, and local agencies
- secure staff employment
- schedule and place staff
- deal with concerns, problems, or dissension among staff and/or parents in an open and caring manner
- work diligently to solve problems as quickly and as fairly as possible for the good of all concerned
- prepare and maintain *all* records
- secure repairs and maintenance

- secure janitorial services
- keep *all* records required by the state
- prepare necessary files for each child
- order supplies and equipment
- maintain school inventory of material and equipment
- obtain adequate insurance
- prepare regulations for disaster procedures
- keep staff records up to date
- maintain a referral system for children with special needs
- assist school board in policy decisions, staff needs, and job descriptions
- be aware of all legal aspects and liabilities—keeping accurate records of accidents, etc.
- maintain all equipment to meet safety codes
- ascertain proper health standards in preparation and serving of food
- assure open and trustful parent-staff relations
- maintain confidential records for each child

EDUCATIONAL

The director is required to:

- ascertain the correct educational curriculum for children according to age and ability
- plan a curriculum that meets the purpose of the school
- provide an educational program appropriate for the children
- guide teachers in the selection of appropriate activities (field trips, visiting, lectures, etc.) for each child's age and ability
- plan and ascertain correct schedules, programs, and routines for children with each teacher
- provide evaluation instruments in relation to a child's progress, development, and special needs
- provide nutritionally sound snacks and meals
- provide programs to inform parents of correct/current educational techniques and trends
- provide valid parent education instructions

STAFF DEVELOPMENT

The director is required to:

- provide programs for professional staff growth
- provide a professional library for staff
- read current research and developments in the early childhood education field
- provide for staff development
- plan participation for staff in workshops, conferences, etc.
- participate in appropriate professional organizations
- prepare job descriptions
- recruit, interview, and secure proper staff
- orient new staff
- provide in-service training for staff
- conduct monthly staff meetings
- keep confidential staff records
- evaluate each staff member annually
- conduct staff development training
- provide for regular staff supervision

CONTRACT

The director is required to:

- determine salary schedule for staff, whether on a nine- or twelve-month schedule
- determine the director's working schedule in conjunction with the school board (nine or twelve months)
- determine benefits to be paid the staff

Supervision of the Director

Supervision is not controlling, checking, or watching. The school board and director must work together for the good of the school. At regular monthly meetings, the board should determine the effectiveness of the director by the reports he/she makes. Thus, regular monthly meetings are a must for the correct administration of the program and its policies. These meetings are also a time when differing viewpoints can be worked out for the good of the school. A school board should not allow a director to be in total control at all times. The board should be a policy-making body, not a puppet of the director. Consequently, the director is responsible for implementing school board policies and procedures. The supervision and evaluation of the director should be predicated on his/her ability to carry out board policies. Therefore, the board should not become involved in the day-to-day operation of the school.

In addition to supervising, the board has a responsibility to work with the director in a spirit of helpfulness and mutual respect. The director's responsibilities are very much like those of a principal, a business executive, and a counselor all combined into one, and the stress can be tremendous. A school board that realizes the pressure in the director's position will take steps to alleviate burnout, which unfortunately is very common in preschool directors. Parents and the community see the director as the spokesperson for the school, and dedication to its purpose must be foremost in his/her mind for the good of the program. Without the support of the board, without periodic rewards and understanding, this dedication can erode in even the most enthusiastic person. If a director has burned out or become ineffective, it is necessary that the board take immediate action to discuss the problems and either solve them or dismiss the director in a legal manner. However, the best way to ensure a director's longevity and effectiveness is not to wait until the last minute, but to provide a constant sense of support and respect from the very start, continuing particularly when the going gets rough.

Summary

The director's job is one of extreme importance and influence. The board's selection must be carefully and professionally determined. The board should not rush through this process, but allow time for careful consideration of the applicants. When the board is well-prepared and knowledgeable of the school's purpose and policies, its members can choose a director who is dedicated to these ideals.

The three most important characteristics for directors are:

(1) They must be professional.
(2) They must love children.
(3) They must learn to trust themselves.

With these three guidelines, a director can operate a professional, loving, and caring program that parents will (by word of mouth) help keep filled.

CHAPTER FOUR

Financial Considerations

IF YOU BUILT CASTLES IN THE AIR,
YOUR WORK NEED NOT BE LOST;
THAT IS WHERE THEY SHOULD BE.
NOW PUT FOUNDATIONS UNDER THEM.

—Henry David Thoreau

ONE of the first questions to be asked will be, "Where is the money coming from to start the program?" In order to determine the answer, a prospective school must first develop a list of income sources. Figure 7 shows a form which could be followed.

In most programs, tuition and fees represent the major income, with fundraising conducted by the school a close second. In small operations, where no additional income can be generated, the program should be self-supporting from the beginning. If this is the case, a quality program can still be developed and operated.

Start-up program costs do not have to be high. Most programs can begin with less than $1,000, if the money is used wisely. Many items needed can be made or purchased in used condition, then upgraded and repaired. Donations of used toys, books, records, tapes, games, etc., can be solicited from individuals or the community. Visit area garage sales—many good items can be found at a fraction of the original cost. However, be sure to check these items for safety and appropriateness to the age of the children that will be using them.

Public school auctions are also a great place to look for tables (27″ high), chairs (15–18″ high), and teacher cabinets. Sometimes Head Start programs replace their equipment, selling their old items at a reduced cost. A little cleanup and repair is often all that is needed.

Churches may be replacing or removing nursery equipment that is no longer needed. Records and books can be checked out from the public library on a thirty-day teacher's pass. This provides varied titles throughout the year.

Source: _____

Amount: _____

Percentage: _____

Tuition, Fees
(Congregational Assistance)

    Gifts: _____

    Fundraising: _____

    Other Income: _____

  Total: _____

Figure 7. Example of funding source list.

Oftentimes department stores replace cabinets and display cases, which can be used for teacher storage or as shelving within rooms. Used computer paper can be used for painting, pasting, etc. Imagination is all that is needed. Many newspapers will also give various forms and sizes of newsprint to schools.

Conserve money for consumable items such as construction paper, crayons, paste, ditto paper, etc. These items will be the largest school expense, except for staff salaries. The best way to offset the expense for consumable items is to charge a supply fee, which is discussed in detail later.

Carpet squares, wallpaper books, Christmas card display folders, etc., are all available free or at minimum cost. Plasterboard bulletin boards can be made very inexpensively, or–if the walls in the room are made of drywall–borders can be stapled to the wall to make bulletin boards. When the wall is painted, all holes will disappear. Bulletin board material can be made, or you can ask department stores for displays that are no longer needed. Usually, store managers will gladly give these displays for use in schools. Never hesitate to ask for these items; store managers can only say no, but most of the time, they will be glad to give the school items that are going to be thrown away. Remember, teachers are natural "packrats." This is a great asset–be proud of it, and have the skills.

There are also many grants available for starting an early

childhood education program. Private individuals also give financial assistance to these types of programs. A good place to start looking for grant information is the public library.

Income

REGISTRATION FEE

The school will probably charge a small registration fee at the time of enrollment. This fee holds a place for the child for the coming school year and is nonrefundable, even if the parent decides to withdraw the child. This registration fee can be used as "start-up" money to begin the program.

Typically, the registration fee is $15–40 per child. The amount charged will be determined by comparing the registration fees of other area preschools. Fees should be kept as close to those charged by surrounding schools as possible, enabling a new program to be competitive. Some programs charge both the registration fee and first semester supply fee at enrollment. The school board will need to decide which method is best, and incorporate the decision into their school policies.

SUPPLY FEES

Because of the high cost of consumable items, most preschools are now charging an annual or per-semester supply fee to supplement the program's income. The supply fee should be determined by the age of child and the number of days per week the child attends. An example is shown in Figure 8.

Program Enrolled	Supply Fee
2 days per week	$20 per semester
3 days per week	$23 per semester
4 days per week	$25 per semester
5 days per week	$28 per semester
Kindergarten (5 half days/week)	$28 per semester

Figure 8. Example of supply fees.

A per-semester supply fee is collected with the first month's tuition and with the January tuition. This method gives the program income twice a year to help cover expenses. Collecting a supply fee twice a year also enables the school to spread income throughout the program year.

TUITION

Tuition is the major income source for the program, and its distribution needs to be carefully monitored.

Collection

Tuition can be collected monthly (easiest method), once per semester, or annually. Most programs use the monthly method because it is the most affordable to parents. A date needs to be set for tuition collection—the first of the month, tenth of the month, etc. The due date for tuition should be included in the parents' school handbook.

Policy

A written school board policy should be developed outlining the procedure the program follows when parents are late paying fees. A policy is definitely necessary because sooner or later problems involving the collection of fees will be experienced by all preschool programs. An example of this is given in Figure 9.

Give an explanation to parents concerning the use of fees, so that they understand from the beginning their actual use within the program. This can be done by means of a letter, such as the one shown in Figure 10.

Late Fees Payment

Late notices regarding fee payments should be sent when accounts are seven days past due. These notices should be mailed directly to parents or sent home with the child. Remember, there are circumstances that a director must consider when

Tuition is based on the actual cost of operating the school. Fees are based on a total year cost for each child, divided into nine equal payments, due on or before the first day of each month, beginning September 1st.

Credit for a child's prolonged illness or emergency can be arranged through the director. No credit is given for vacations or holidays.

A registration fee is due when the child is enrolled. A supply fee (determined by class enrollment) is due on or before the September payment.

Two consecutive months of delinquent tuition payment will result in the child's automatic withdrawal from the school rolls, unless arrangements have been made with the director.

Figure 9. Sample tuition policy.

RE: Tuition and Supply Fee

Dear Parents,

Some of you have had questions as to the use of your monthly tuition and supply fee. I appreciate your questions and hope the following will help you understand our finances.

MONTHLY TUITION

Tuition is used to pay for staff salaries, repayment of the loan for the building remodeling and additions, payment of loan for major equipment purchases, and unexpected purchases for classrooms.

SUPPLY FEE

The supply fee is used for insurance costs, which have risen sharply in the past two years; consumable materials (paint, construction paper, pencils, paste, crayons, glue, and items too numerous to list); paper supplies (toilet paper, paper towels, kleenex, cups, etc.); snacks; new toys and classroom equipment; educational programs; offices; and so on.

If you have additional questions or comments, I'll be happy to discuss them with you.

Sincerely,

Director

Figure 10. Sample letter to parents concerning fees, ABC Preschool.

an account is overdue. Parents may have several good reasons for delaying payment of the account. The director's responsibility is to contact parents to discuss reasons for nonpayment and to offer a solution that is in the mutual best interest of the child and the school. This is a business, so react in a business-like manner, but take the time and effort to determine the validity of the parent's reason(s). However, one must always remember that the school's mission is to serve the child—never lose sight of the *reason* for the school's existence. There may be parents who will habitually be late in their payments. If so, such parents must be dealt with authoritatively. Figure 11 shows a sample late payment notice.

Accounts that are two weeks or more past due should be contacted by telephone or by registered mail, as shown in Figure 12.

If an account still remains unpaid, the matter should be brought before the school board. The board is then responsible for sending a registered letter to the parent (by mail), stating the policies and action that will be taken if the bill remains unpaid, or what course the parents are to take if they wish the child to remain in the program. This letter might follow the pattern shown in Figure 13.

An account that is not paid for two consecutive months should result in automatic withdrawal of the child from the program, unless arrangements are made with the director and the board.

There are times when it may be necessary to turn accounts over to a legal advisor for collection. The school board will need to determine the policies and procedures the director should follow in regard to delinquent accounts.

Determining Costs

Tuition cost will be determined largely by comparable surrounding school fees. Other schools will usually quote their rates and prices. Fees can then be determined, within a suitable range, according to the price structure of other schools. A listing such as the one shown in Figure 14 should be prepared.

```
┌─────────────────────────────────────────────────────────┐
│                OVERDUE PAYMENT NOTICE                   │
│                                                         │
│  Child's Name: _____  │
│                                                         │
│  Dear Parent,                                           │
│                                                         │
│     Tuition for the month of _____ in the amount │
│  of _____ is now _____ days past due. │
│  Please remit immediately.                              │
│                                                         │
│  Sincerely,                                             │
│                                                         │
│  Director                                               │
└─────────────────────────────────────────────────────────┘
```

Figure 11. Sample notice of late payment.

```
┌─────────────────────────────────────────────────────────┐
│                OVERDUE PAYMENT NOTICE                   │
│                                                         │
│  Date: _____ │
│                                                         │
│  Child's Name: _____  │
│                                                         │
│  Dear Parents,                                          │
│                                                         │
│     As of the above date, we have not received the following pay- │
│  ment for the month of _____:         │
│                                                         │
│       Tuition  _____  │
│                         (amount due)                    │
│                                                         │
│       Supply Fee  _____  │
│                                                         │
│  Please remit on your child's next class time.          │
│                                                         │
│  Sincerely,                                             │
│                                                         │
│  Director                                               │
└─────────────────────────────────────────────────────────┘
```

Figure 12. Example of second notice of late payment.

Date: _____

Child's Name: _____

Dear Parents,

Our accounting records indicate that you currently owe the school $_____. Please remit said amount to the school immediately or contact the director if there is some problem or question concerning this account.

Thank you in advance for your prompt attention and anticipated cooperation in the matter.

Sincerely,

Director

Chair, School Board

Figure 13. Sample of board letter for nonpayment.

TUITION AND SUPPLY FEE SCHEDULE

Our rates are as follows:

Registration Fee for every child when entering the school—$20.00.

Tuition is paid by the month, and Supply Fee is paid by the semester (September and January).

# Class Days per Week	Tuition	Supply (Sept. & Jan.)
2	$30.00	$20.00
3	$40.00	$23.00
4	$50.00	$25.00
Kindergarten (5 half-days)	$55.00	$28.00

Figure 14. Example of fees charged, ABC Preschool.

Families with two or more children pay the regular fees for each child (there is no cost break for more children). Recording and handling of the fees will be discussed in detail later.

Budget Planning

Plan realistically for the program's finances. Take time to chart carefully a sound, realistic budget. Plan for the unexpected, and keep in mind that it is better to overestimate than to underestimate financial needs. Remember, these are projections, not concrete spending amounts, so plan accordingly. A significant part of budget planning is determining the date for beginning the fiscal year. At ABC Preschool we use August 1 to July 31; other programs use January 1 to December 31, or July 1 to June 30. ABC Preschool uses the August 1 to July 31 fiscal year because the school board can set a realistic budget that will project a school year's expenditures and receipts. The school board should determine a fiscal date that is easiest for program budget development.

The Budget

A budget generally includes numerous categories. Figure 15 illustrates sample budget categories with percentages that are given as guidelines and will change slightly from year to year and from school to school.

Special Budget Considerations

DIRECTOR'S SALARY

The director's salary should reflect his/her professional background, experience, and responsibilities. A director often works as many hours at home as he/she does at school. The director attends meetings and workshops, plans and implements parent programs, buys supplies, does bookkeeping, keeps accurate child's records, cleans, builds, etc. The direc-

Budget Items	Percent of Budget
Staff Salaries	65.0%
Staff Benefits	3.5%
Equipment	5.0%
Consumable Supplies	7.0%
Snacks	3.0%
Office Supplies/Phone	3.5%
Insurance	1.5%
Cleaning Services	1.0%
Licenses/Dues	.5%
Parent Education	.5%
Scholarships	1.0%
Conferences, Consultants, Workshops	1.5%
Miscellaneous	1.0%
Utilities	1.0%
Rent or Cost of Mortgage	6.0%
TOTAL	100.00%

Figure 15. Sample budget categories, ABC Preschool.

tor's salary should reflect these added hours, either by salary or by fringe benefits. In effect, the director is paid for the level of responsibility, not the actual number of hours worked.

TEACHERS' SALARIES

Teachers also should receive benefits and salaries that reflect their professional abilities. Often teachers' salaries will reflect the marketplace. If there is an abundance of teachers in the area, early childhood programs can often employ teachers at less than competitive school districts. Conversely, if a teacher shortage exists, the school may be forced to pay salaries comparable to surrounding public school systems.

WORKMAN'S COMPENSATION INSURANCE

Workman's Compensation Insurance and Social Security payments are required by law and must be included in salary schedules, if staff are contracted by the school. If, however, staff are self-employed, check with local revenue offices (federal and state) for specific laws governing these circumstances.

FRINGE BENEFITS

Sick leave, vacation days, personal days, and medical insurance need to be considered within the budget as well as funds to assist staff members in continuing their education. A substitute teacher pay scale should also be addressed in budget planning.

All of the above must be considered when determining a realistic operating budget. Enrollment projections for the coming year should give a preliminary revenue picture for budget planning. If the enrollment projections are realistically determined, the board will have a sound basis for budget planning. The director and school board should examine the fee structure and make a determination as to whether fees should be increased to generate additional income for the next year. Inflation will also need to be considered in the formulation of the next year's budget.

A budget has to be well-planned and projected accurately. Careful consideration of both income and disbursements are necessary before a realistic budget can be formulated. Accurate bookkeeping records from previous years are essential in planning a budget, as they provide the school board with a detailed account of all expenditure and revenue areas. Three essential components of good budget planning for a preschool program are:

(1) It allows adequate time for planning.

(2) It is realistic in enrollment and distribution projections.

(3) It keeps accurate financial records.

Management

The school board will decide who is responsible for handling the program's finances. The following is a list of possibilities:

(1) Director is totally responsible.

(2) Director receives income; bookkeeper deposits income and pays expenditures, keeping all records.

(3) Director receives and deposits income; bookkeeper pays expenditures and keeps ledgers.

(4) Bookkeeper is totally responsible.

There are many variations for determining financial responsibilities. The school board must decide which plan is best suited for the program. However, for best accountability, some form of checks and balances must be used. A designated system of checks and balances will also simplify state and federal tax records.

Salary Schedule

The staff salary schedule will be the largest and most important budget item. The school board should determine a base pay scale for all employees. Teachers' salaries will be determined by education, experience, and contact teaching hours per week. Teacher assistants' salaries are usually based on minimum wage as a beginning point. See Figure 16 for a sample salary schedule.

Some preschools treat their staff as employees contracted for service. This means that the school considers a staff member as self-employed. In contracting staff in this manner, the staff member is responsible for his/her own taxes, thus relieving the school of tax responsibilities. Check with the local Internal Revenue Service office for the forms needed to provide for employment verification for contract employees on their tax returns.

A salary schedule can range from 60 to 75 percent of the total budget, depending on funding income. Unfortunately, early childhood education staff and directors are often paid very minimal salaries. Any preschool program is only as good as the staff. If high salaries are not possible, attempt to give other fringe benefits to the staff. Dinners, small gifts, attendance at workshops, conferences, staff children attending the program free of charge, special recognition in the community, etc., are examples of some benefits given in lieu of salary.

ABC PRESCHOOL SALARY SCHEDULE

This salary schedule is based on 80% of what a first year teacher makes in the _____ public school system.

These are beginning salaries and years of experience must be added to the levels.

DIRECTOR:

Full day (7:30 A.M.–3:00 P.M.) five (5) days per week twelve (12) months per year.

B.S. Degree	$12,000–$14,000
M.A. Degree	$16,000–$19,000

TEACHERS:

No Degree	$14.00 half day
B.S. Degree	$17.00 half day
M.A. Degree	$20.00 half day
Kindergarten	$23.00 half day

Salaries are based on a half day. If the teacher works a full day the salary is doubled.

Teacher's assistant: Federal and state minimum wage per hour.

Figure 16. Sample salary schedule.

Always include in each year's budget a salary increase, no matter how small, as a reward to the staff for a job well done.

Tax Sheets for Staff

Accurate and confidential pay records must be kept for each staff member. These records include all tax information, social security number, length of pay period (nine or twelve months), personal information concerning staff, etc.

A sample personnel record is shown in Figure 17. These forms can be purchased at a local office supply store and are continually updated. Each staff member should have a completed form in their personal files.

Income Ledger Sheets

An income ledger such as that shown in Figure 18 must be kept on each child to show the amount and date of payment. These ledger sheets can be arranged by class or individual child. Experience has shown it is easiest to arrange by class, permitting the entire year's payment and class records of enrollment to be used in future planning.

Monthly Financial Reports

For the program to run smoothly it is necessary to prepare and analyze each month's receipts and expenditures. The typical program has two forms the school board reviews each month.

ACCOUNTS RECEIVABLE LEDGER

This budget sheet, shown in Figure 19, illustrates the beginning balance from the previous month, plus a listing of each class by age, with the number of children paid for the reporting month, free tuition children, and total tuition paid for each class that month. Included is a column for supply fee collected in September and January (this section will only be completed during these months, unless there are new enrollees). Accounts unpaid are marked and totalled. Receipts other than tuition are listed and totalled, giving total ledger receipts. This information is taken from the income ledger sheets for each child and class.

The bottom half shows total deposits for the month. Also listed will be refunds, returned checks, and cash transactions. Each of the areas are totalled and subtracted from the total deposits, giving the amount used for total adjusted deposits, which must equal the amount found under total ledger receipts.

There is also a space for savings account balance. This account is used to deposit summer salary funds during the school year. This account will be used to pay staff during the summer months. Further information will be given concerning summer pay.

```
Name: _____  Social Security #: _____
Address: _____
Date of Birth: _____  Phone No.: _____

                                    Date              Date
    Position          Rate         Started          Terminated
  _____      _____    _____      _____

  _____      _____    _____      _____

Remarks: _____
_____

Pay on twelve-month scale _____

                    First Quarter 19___

Week #: _____     Rate: _____     Total: _____
                                     Total Net: _____

Tax Deductions:

FICA: _____     Federal: _____     State: _____
COT: _____     Ded.: _____      Pay: _____
Check #: _____         Dated: _____
```

Figure 17. Sample personnel record, ABC Preschool.

```
Class  03–three year olds
Time  Monday–Wednesday A.M.
Child's Name  Jane Doe     Paid
```

Permission Slip	Registration Fee	Sept. Supply	Sept. Tuition
X	4/26	8/25	9/1
	$20.00	$20.00	$32.00

*The example illustrates September. The ledger will ultimately reflect the entire school year.
(A twelve-column ledger sheet in paperback book form can be used to store this information.)

Figure 18. Example of student ledger sheet, ABC Preschool.

PRESCHOOL FINANCIAL REPORT

Beginning Balance: _____

Receipts for Month of: _____

Accounts Receivable Ledger

Number of Fee Paid Children	Class	Free Tuition	Supply Total
_____	Three's Younger	_____	_____
_____	Four's Regular	_____	_____
_____	Four's Pre-K	_____	_____
_____	Kindergarten	_____	_____
_____	TOTALS	_____	_____

Account Unpaid: _____

Receipts other than tuition: _____
  (amount)

Source: _____

Total Ledger Receipts

Total Deposits:	_____
Refunds:	_____
Returned Checks:	_____
Cash Transactions:	_____
Total Adjusted Deposits:	_____
Savings Accounts Balance:	_____

Figure 19. Sample financial report, ABC Preschool.

ACCOUNTS PAYABLE LEDGER

This form, shown in Figure 20, is taken from the account ledger, which shows all deposits and expenditures.

This balance sheet will give the board an ongoing account of receipts and expenditures and also provide a model for budget planning. Balance sheets should be done monthly, a copy should be provided to the school board, and copies retained for financial records. Miscellaneous expenditures should be itemized and listed for the school board's records. Remember, all bookkeeping records need to be kept for seven years for the Internal Revenue Service's purposes.

Yearly Financial Statement

At the close of the school year (or fiscal year) a statement of receipts and expenditures can be prepared. This statement will provide a comparison between amounts budgeted and actual expenditures. The yearly financial statement will serve as a guide in preparing next year's budget. An example is shown in Figure 21.

Taxes

TAX-EXEMPT STATUS

Application for tax-exempt status must be made to the Internal Revenue Service if the program is a nonprofit organization. If the program is associated with a church (as a part of that church), then the church's tax-exempt number can be used. To apply for tax-exempt status, contact the local Internal Revenue Service (I.R.S.) office to obtain an application and filing form.

FEDERAL TAXES

If the preschool program is operated within a church, the church's federal tax identification number can be used. How-

Balance Sheet for:	MONTH	
Balance on hand:		
Deposits:		
TOTAL:		
Expenditures for:	MONTH	
Check No.	To Whom	Amount
Total Expenditures:		
Balance on hand:		

Figure 20. Sample accounts payable ledger, ABC Preschool.

FINANCIAL STATEMENT FOR YEAR

Credits
  Tuition   _____
  Supplies   _____
  Fundraisers   _____
           TOTALS   _____

Debit
  Salaries   _____
  FICA, SIT, FIT, COT   _____
  Sub. Teachers   _____
  Cleaning   _____
  Equipment   _____
  Insurance   _____
  Supplies   _____
  ACT (loan payment)   _____
  Miscellaneous   _____
  Mileage Expenses   _____
  Service Charge   _____
  Services (bookkeeping)   _____
  Director (part
  summer salary)   _____
           TOTALS   _____

Outstanding Debts
  Loan (XXXX)   _____
  Loan (XXX)   _____
  Remainder of Director
  Summer Salary   _____
           TOTALS   _____

Figure 21. Sample yearly financial statement, ABC Preschool.

Employee Name: _____

Monthly Salary	FICA	Matching	Total
_____	_____	_____	_____

The employer pays the matched amount, so the total paid is employee _____% and employer _____%.

Figure 22. Example of social security tax.

ever, contact the I.R.S. prior to operation of the program to inform them of the program addition for their files.

If the program is not operated in conjunction with a church, a separate federal tax identification number is required. The appropriate forms can be obtained from the local I.R.S. office.

SOCIAL SECURITY TAX

Social Security taxes must be paid on each employee. This tax is matched dollar for dollar by the employer. See Figure 22 for an example of the form.

This tax (FICA-Social Security) is deposited monthly along with FIT (Federal Income Tax) and reported quarterly on the employer's quarterly tax return. I.R.S. Circular E–Employer's Tax Guide–contains tax tables that specify withholding FICA and FIT tax amounts.

STATE TAXES

Each state is unique in the collection of employee state income tax (SIT). In fact, some states do not currently have a state income tax. Obtain a state withholding tax booklet containing instructions for employers and withholding tax tables from an accountant or the State Finance Department. Quarterly tax forms for reporting withholding and payments to the state should be obtained and promptly submitted. State tax number for reporting should be filed in a manner similar to the federal tax information.

CITY TAXES

Many municipal areas are now withholding city taxes, and a city occupational tax (COT). These taxes are usually withheld from the employee's pay according to a percentage of the gross income. These taxes are also reported quarterly to the municipality where the program is located. They are also reported annually by gross yearly income and tax withheld.

General Information

One person should be designated to complete the payroll, calculate taxes, and sign and complete tax information for the preschool. This person should be knowledgeable concerning current tax information and have authorization from the school board to pay and sign tax forms. Tax information must be accurate and records must be current. All records must be kept for seven years as governed by the I.R.S.

All tax information should be kept up to date and quarterly forms should be completed and returned on time. The chart in Figure 23 gives a general idea of what is due when. Monthly federal deposits must be made before the last day of the month in which the tax was withheld. At the end of the year (December 31), all employee tax information must be totalled and transferred to W-2 forms to be given to each employee. Copies of the W-2 need to be sent to federal, state, and local tax services, along with federal transmittal forms, state employee records, and city transmittal records. W-2 forms and all federal, state, and local transmittal forms and copies of W-2's must be distributed to employees and sent to respective agencies prior to January 31.

Computer Use

The use of a micro-computer for record keeping in time savings will be astronomical. Many software programs are available that will handle not only financial concerns, but general staff and student data. Check with local computer dealers for current costs.

Summary

The financial portion of the program will be of great importance and concern, but it is important to remember the "vision" with which planning began. Give the program two or three years to get established; don't "bail out" before giving it a fair chance. With time and planning, finances will fall into

Date Filed	Form	Reason
First Organized	#1023 Tax-Exempt Application	Nonprofit corporation tax exempt
	SS-4 Employer's federal reports	I.D. No. all I.D. No.
	904 Unemployment (not needed if tax-exempt)	Federal Tax
	State I.D. No.	I.D. for all state reports
New Employees	W-4 Withholding Exemption Certificate	Statement of employee's exemptions
Date varies with amount	501 Federal Deposit Receipts	To deposit with Depository Bank withheld funds
March 31 June 30 Sept. 30 Dec. 31	Employer's Quarterly Return for Federal State and City	To report to each agency withholdings from employees
Jan. 31	W-2 Federal, State, Local Wage Tax Statement	Employee's use for filing tax returns
Jan. 31	W-3 Transmittal Reconciliation of Federal, State, and Local taxes	Reconciliation forms for summary of employee tax

Figure 23. Financial forms.

place and the seeds that were planted will take form. Remember to be realistic and conservative in the plans. Everything doesn't need to be the "best," but it needs to be well-prepared and safe. Start small, and build as it becomes possible. A tiny acorn doesn't become an oak overnight.

Matching funds are available through varied sources. Be creative and always maintain a positive outlook. Reports are a vital part of this section of the program. Good report forms help to describe more clearly the financial weaknesses or strengths, and give a total financial outlook quickly. Monthly reporting is a check on the financial books assisting in proper recording, payment of bills, and depositing. Monthly reporting also gives an immediate indication of when spending is exceeding income. The board should always require monthly financial reports and a yearly audit of the books.

Proper management of finances can produce an excellent program even on a shoestring budget. Again, remember to take time in preparing a budget, be realistic with income and expenditure amounts, and keep current and accurate records. These three suggestions will save time, energy, and headaches. There will be good years and bad years, so be prepared for both; by doing this you will enjoy the wonderful benefits and growing experiences that will strengthen the program.

CHAPTER FIVE

The Facility

THE REALITY OF THE BUILDING DOES NOT CONSIST IN THE
ROOF AND WALLS, BUT IN THE SPACE WITHIN TO BE LIVED IN.
—Lao-Tzu

THE director would be wise to take a full inventory of the school facility. The classrooms available, outdoor space, bathroom facilities, and kitchen area should be analyzed. Look for needed repairs, previous improvements, exits, lighting, ventilation, furnace and air-conditioning, flooring type, wall preparations, and fire alarm system. One of the first steps in facility planning is having the state fire marshall's office inspect the building to determine requirements necessary to ensure the facility meets child safety standards. Remember to write down the state fire marshall's stated improvements, and have the fire marshall sign the document. Officials often have a tendency to change their minds, so get the report in writing to ensure a permanent record of the visit and recommendations for improvement.

Safety regulations will definitely require smoke alarms (or a fire alarm system) and fire extinguishers. Fire extinguishers must meet certain standards and types. Find out the exact requirements from the fire marshall. Also, the facility speaks for the program quality: space, safety, and eye pleasure will be an important part of a parent's first impression.

Building Requirements

Most state regulations require a minimum of thirty-five square feet of space per child. This required space is actual use space, excluding hallways, bathrooms, storage, and kitchen. Space is calculated as a whole rather than individually for each room. There may be small classrooms and a large open

43

Classroom = 36 × 40
Restroom = 24 × 14
Multi-purpose Classroom = 24 × 20
Classroom = 20 × 20
Hall = 80 feet
Total floor square feet = 3,200 square feet
Total child space (exclude bath and hall) = 2,656 square feet
Square feet (2656) ÷ 35 = # of children (75.89) or 76 children
*This formula gives the number of children possible per useable total square footage.

Figure 24. Example of space requirements formula.

area, but the total square footage divided by thirty-five gives the number of children the center is licensed to accommodate. Figure 24 shows an example of calculating the maximum number of children allowed.

Requirements for toilet facilities include one lavatory and one commode for every twenty children. The example illustrated should have four commodes and four lavatories, permitting licensure for up to eighty children. There must also be a given number of outside exits for fire requirements. (Check with the state fire marshall for specific regulations.) Walls and floor coverings are also required to meet specific state fire code standards. All of these requirements are determined by the fire marshall and local health department. Be sure to get these inspections at the beginning of program planning, because a center may not open prior to passing these inspections.

Outdoor Requirements

The requirement for outdoor space is seventy-two square feet per child. The playground should be large enough for twenty children at a time, or 1,440 square feet. This area should be fenced for safety with "No Trespassing" signs around the perimeter (for liability insurance) and locked. The surface area should be covered with grass, sand, or a material that will provide a safe surface for children to run and play. Asphalt or concrete provides a smooth surface for riding toys, but is dangerous for swings and climbing equipment. A mixture of surfaces is better, so all areas will be safe for play. Gravel is not a suitable surface for outdoor space because it is difficult for riding toys and unsafe for swings, running, etc.

Figure 25 gives a good view of a sample play area. A sandbox (old tire) is a must in any play area; scoops, sieves, trucks, tractors, etc., should also be included for creative play. Old tires can be partially buried and used for climbing, jumping, and bouncing. If old tires are used, bury tires standing up. Swings, climbing equipment, etc., should be sturdy and age-appropriate. Equipment does not have to be elaborate, but it must have a smooth surface and be safe.

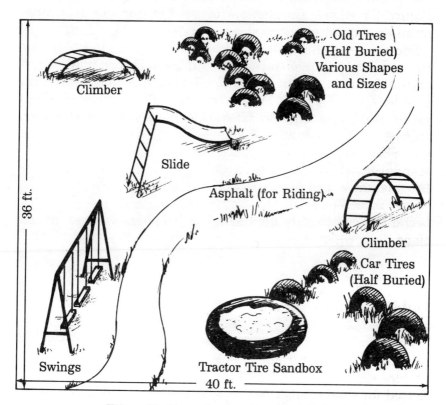

Figure 25. *Example of a playground area.*

Shade trees in the playground area can provide relief from the sun, but can also present safety problems. Children have a natural climbing sense, so bottom limbs should be removed to eliminate the possibility of climbing injuries.

Fencing around the playground area should be high enough to prevent children from climbing into the playground when school is not in session. Remember, the school is liable if someone gets hurt even if they were not authorized to be on the playground. Since the fence is a visible hazard, the fence should consist of solid boards if possible, rather than chain link. With the board fence people outside cannot see what is inside, and thus will be less tempted to enter the play area. Also a board fence is very difficult to climb. There should be a gate(s) to the playground, which should be kept locked when the playground is not in use.

Children using the play area are to be supervised at *all* times—never leave the children alone. Teachers should schedule and rotate playground times permitting all the children to have ample play space.

At the beginning of the year teach the children playground rules! The rules will be determined according to the program and the facility. Figure 26 provides a sample list. Remember, *safety* is first and foremost when the children utilize the playground.

Classroom Climate

The classroom's "child-inviting" atmosphere will be judged by parents when they are assessing the quality of the school

---

(1) Toys are to remain in specified areas.
(2) Sand should not be thrown.
(3) When running, swinging, climbing, etc., watch for other children in the area.
(4) Fighting is not permitted.
(5) Share the toys.

Figure 26. Example of playground rules.

program. Everything in the room should be child-sized, and at a child's level of sight. One way to get a child's view of the room is to get on your knees and observe the room at their height. Children need to be able to reach and put away things themselves.

Everything children use in the room should be at their "grasping level." Bright, pleasant colors should be used, but not loud colors. The room should be fun, educational, safe, interesting, and enjoyable for each child. A feeling of love and warmth should flow from the room, along with caring and safety. The classroom should provide a place to which children want to return.

The classroom should have enough space to allow movement that is easy and flowing. There should be areas for quiet and play time. Room for growth should be planned, and pathways for easy transition should be included. A good room size is determined by square footage. There should be approximately thirty-five square feet per child, but it can be less if another room is being used for active play. A room of 700 square feet will accommodate twenty children.

Check ventilation, heating, cooling, and light to make certain they are adequate. Classrooms can get very warm with eighteen to twenty active bodies giving off heat. Measure the rooms and determine the class size to calculate the number of children that can be adequately served. Floor coverings should be appropriate to the area's use. Vinyl should be included for "messy activities" areas, the halls, and the bathrooms. Carpet is best suited for "reading areas" and "library."

Interest Centers

Centers are the most important part of the classroom. They include these areas: art, science, blocks, books, dramatic play, messy activities (paint, water, cooking, etc.), sensory activities, music, woodworking, and manipulative games and toys.

When planning these centers, define areas by the different types of activities: messy, active, quiet, small group, and large group. The art area should be near water, and requires a washable floor. The block area should be large, carpeted to reduce noise, and away from the pathways of children moving within the room. Other areas are arranged in the space remaining, keeping in mind their purpose and requirements. For example, the library area should have good lighting, electrical outlets for a record player, and an aquarium pump. Keep in mind also that the overall arrangement must enable adults to observe children's activities throughout the classroom.

Some teachers use a pocket system for moving from center to center. Library pockets for the number of children allowed in a center at one time are placed on the wall or table next to each center. Children have keys with their names on them, which they place in the pocket of the desired center. When all pockets are filled no one else can enter that center. When a child leaves the center he/she takes the key out of the pocket and moves to another center with available space. This procedure lets a teacher control the number of children in a center at any one time. There are other methods of moving children from center to center; experiment to find the one that is most desirable.

Figure 27 is only an example of one way a classroom can be arranged. The room should be set up to accommodate the needs of those using it. Remember to separate areas that are designated for quiet and those for active play.

Equipment

All early childhood rooms require furnishings that support classroom activities and respond to the children's needs. Wood is the favored material for furnishings, but molded plastic equipment is gaining popularity. Furnishings need to be sturdy, attractive, and easily cleaned.

Tables (27″ high) and chairs (15–18″ high) should be proportional to the size of the children using them. Small tables designed for three to four people give greater flexibility than large tables (those designed for eight to ten children). Kidney-shaped tables are nice for teaching small groups, but take up more room than rectangular tables. There should be a space for each child to store his/her personal belongings; some call these cubbyholes, square compartments, or ice cream tubs. These can take up a great deal of space. Experience has found

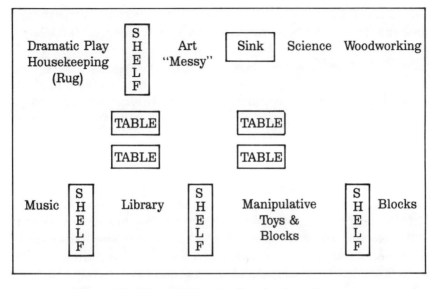

Figure 27. Example of center location in a classroom.

that providing a central place to hang coats and a mailbox for papers works much better. The mailbox is usually 4′ × 4′ with 3″ × 5″ size compartments. The compartments can be as large as desired with a child's name on each.

Shelves should be low and open (easily accessible to children) providing them the responsibility of making choices and returning materials when they are finished. Book shelves need to be provided, which will encourage children to use and care for books.

There must also be adequate storage for materials that adults must closely supervise. Cleaning materials, the teacher's personal property, curriculum guides, children's files, and first-aid materials all need proper storage, either within the classroom or a central storage area.

Equipment should be assessed on how it will influence the children. Good equipment is equipment that is attractive, feels good, is well-constructed, sturdy, in good repair, works properly, and fits a child's abilities and interests. Natural materials such as sand, water, paint, clay, and paper are important materials that should be included in every program. When purchasing materials always evaluate them as to their safety, toxicity, cleanliness, and sensory appeal (color, texture, and smell).

TYPE OF EQUIPMENT AND MATERIALS

Sand, water, and clay provide children with both sensory and mathematical experiences. Children learn about the properties of substances through pouring, feeling, and mixing. Sand and water play areas that are indoors should be in tubs or water tables, and located on washable floors. Woodworking helps develop coordination and skill in using tools and offers challenges in measurement and construction. Tools should be sturdy, child-sized, and well supervised because of sharp edges. Excellent materials to use include styrofoam sheets or wood scraps, which can be obtained from a local planing mill. A tree log is also excellent and inexpensive.

ACTIVE PLAY EQUIPMENT

Equipment for active play offers excellent opportunities for vigorous movement and exploration. Active play helps children develop and explore their physical limits, develop creativity, release energy, and learn many spatial concepts by experiencing them with their own bodies. These materials can be hand-made and rather inexpensive—wooden boxes, tires, planks, tree stumps, climbing apparatus, swings, rockers, seesaws, slides, tricycles, wagons, rolling toys, parachutes— almost anything (use your imagination). The number of these materials is limitless. All of these aid in large muscle coordination, balance, and development. Again, materials should be child-sized and safe.

BLOCKS

These materials are construction toys and include blocks, Legos®, Tinkertoys®, Lincoln Logs®, Ring-Gan-Tiks®, Snap Blocks®, Bristle Blocks®, etc. Blocks are very beneficial in the following ways: they help to develop fine motor coordination and strength; they enhance imagination and creativity; they provide opportunities for children to learn to work and play together; and they provide experiences in problem solving, ratios, and measurement.

Each room should have a full set of unit blocks, either wooden, cardboard, or plastic, which develop construction experiences as well as mathematical relationships. This play is enhanced when toy cars, trucks, trains, and toy human and animal figures are added, because they provide children with the expression of a growing understanding of the real world. Adequate space and storage for blocks will aid in clean-up time. Block rules should be clearly stated and enforced for safety.

MANIPULATIVE MATERIALS

Manipulative materials include the realm of materials designed to give children practice in eye-hand coordination, and help in developing the small muscles of the fingers and hands. These experiences prepare children for writing and expose children to concepts of size, color, and shape, which help in the children's ability to recognize letters and words. Manipulative materials include puzzles (wooden, plastic, and rubber), beads, pegs and peg-boards, Bristle Blocks®, spools, parque blocks, Tinkertoys®, Lincoln Logs®, lacing pads, designs and patterns, sewing cards, feely boxes, classification sets, and many other varied materials. Many of these manipulatives can be made with file folder games, manila folder games, etc. Use your imagination, again—the list is almost limitless.

DRAMATIC PLAY (HOUSEKEEPING)

These materials provide learning experiences and practice in the skills of daily living. In this area, children imitate the actions of adults and older children in their lives by playing out a situation and experiencing the various adult roles. These materials can be organized as an interest center with dress-up clothes (both sexes), kitchen appliances, kitchenware, play food, books, rocking chairs, small dust mop, mop, broom, vacuum, dolls, cradles—the list is almost limitless. Include in this area special interest items—hats and sample clothes of firemen, nurses, policemen, doctors, post office workers, and various other businesses and trades. Other special items can be added: store, restaurant, bus, and fire hoses help children become creative in their thinking and play. Many times children will take a play item and pretend it is something totally different, which will help expand their imaginative realm.

Books

Every room needs an assortment of quality books. The experiences gained from being allowed to touch, hold, and thumb through a book helps a child to discover the joy of reading and helps to motivate the child to want to read. Children not only need to read their own books and have stories read to them, they also need to see adults use and enjoy books. The library area should be comfortable, quiet, and have an ample supply of good quality children's books. These should be displayed at the child's eye-level, and be easily accessible to the child. If there is not enough money to buy a supply of good children's books, check with the library. Books can often be checked out on a thirty-day teacher's pass. Doing this will give the classroom a good range of different books at no expense.

Art Materials

Art materials provide opportunities for creative expression, problem solving, and exploration, and they help a child develop physically and sensorially. Art is the child's work, and should be left as the child did it. Materials should be free form and expressive—clay, collage materials, paints (tempera, bubbles, finger-paint, shaving cream, pudding, etc.), dough, glue, slime, crayons, and pencils. These materials help children to develop concepts and comparisons, and to classify, measure, and relate to others of all ages. In the curriculum unit these materials and their uses will be discussed more fully.

Kitchen (Cooking Area)

Every program needs to have an area used for cooking and snack preparation. This area most likely will be a kitchen, which must be kept clean and sanitized. Food supplies are required to be in cabinets separate from other supplies. For day-care programs the storage doors must be marked to designate school or other use.

State health officials must inspect this area prior to the opening of the school. There must be a carbon dioxide fire extinguisher located in the area, which is available for cooking fires. All cleaning supplies must be kept out of the reach of children, and unless they are doing a cooking activity, children should not be allowed in the kitchen area.

In some cases, cooking can be done in the classroom. Remember, if using electrical appliances, observe extreme caution for the children's safety. Supervision is a must in any cooking activity, rules of safety in using utensils and stoves are necessary and must be enforced. Cooking is a fun and essential activity in an early childhood program, but because of the many hazards, cooking activities must be *well-supervised.*

Storage Area

Every program needs a central storage room in addition to teacher storage within the classroom. This area provides space for bulk storage of snack cups, toilet tissue, snacks, extra toys, paper supplies, glue, paste, office supplies, napkins, etc. The storage area should be accessible to staff only—children should not be allowed in this storage room. The door should remain closed and locked at all times due to safety regulations.

Providing a separate additional storage area gives teachers more space in their classrooms, and also provides a central location for items that all staff members use occasionally. The storage area does not have to be large, but it should contain shelves for proper storage.

Teacher Workroom/Lounge

If possible, an area (it can also be a storage room) should be set aside where teachers can go to work on lesson plans, use copy or ditto machines, the paper cutter, the typewriter, or other office machines. Many new early childhood programs also have a library of teacher resource books. The teacher workroom area gives privacy for the staff and provides space for class preparation. This room should be well lighted and accessible to all the staff. The room can also serve as a staff lunchroom if the staff works all day. A drink machine or refrigerator should be in the room for the staff's convenience. Again, building space will need to be assessed, but providing a workroom/lounge can be a definite plus for the staff by providing an area where they can socialize as well as work. As stated before, salaries are often not as high in early childhood education programs, but other benefits can be offered which will develop positive work and social relationships within the staff.

INVENTORY SHEET		
Teacher: _____		
Date: _____		
Item	Quantity	Condition (+, OK, −)
Chairs	_____	_____
Tables	_____	_____
_____	_____	_____
_____	_____	_____
_____	_____	_____
_____	_____	_____
_____	_____	_____
_____	_____	_____
_____	_____	_____
_____	_____	_____
_____	_____	_____
_____	_____	_____

Comments:
_____
_____
_____

*Items listed herein are the property of ABC Preschool.

Figure 28. Example of an inventory record.

Director's Office

The director's office is the repository for all school records. The director's office should be locked at all times when not in use, because of the confidentiality of school records. The director should be provided with a desk and file cabinets which hold the following files: enrollment, applications, class records, teacher contracts, assignments, payroll, resumes, bookkeeping records, checkbook, children's accounts receivable ledgers, tax information, and other confidential materials. Board reports, policy information, program forms, and letters should be filed in the director's office also.

The director should retain resource materials to keep updated on happenings in the early childhood education area: books and publications from early childhood professional associations and management guides from the field of early childhood education. Inventory lists of all materials housed within the classrooms, storage room, teacher workroom, and general areas of the facility and play area are also kept in the director's office. An example of such an inventory sheet is shown in Figure 28.

CHAPTER SIX

Enrollment

KEEP THY SHOP AND THY SHOP WILL KEEP THEE.
—Ben Jonson

ENROLLMENT is one of the most important concerns when setting up a preschool program, because without enrollment the best program cannot operate. This section is divided into ten specified areas, which are discussed in detail.

Recruitment

There are many forms of recruitment, each of which is valid.

ADVERTISEMENT

This form of recruitment will be necessary for a beginning program and can be done by newspaper, radio, or television. Each of these types of media is expensive, therefore wise use of space and time is essential.

Make sure the newspaper advertisement is brief, to the point, and eye pleasing. Figure 29 shows an example. Do not crowd a lot of words into a small space. Give the ad character and be specific. Give two phone numbers if possible, for registration information.

A sign should also be erected at the school giving the information shown in Figure 30.

PARENT LETTERS

Recruitment can also be accomplished by a letter to the parents of the children that are enrolled (in January for the next year, or throughout the year if enrollment is down) stat-

57

ENROLLING FOR FALL

ABC Preschool

Ages Three Years–Kindergarten
A Loving Preschool
State Certified
Specializing in Early Development Programs

To Enroll Call—555-0000
Monday–Friday (8 A.M.–2 P.M.)

Figure 29. Sample newspaper ad.

ing that enrollment applications are being accepted. Parents can also be asked to share this enrollment letter with a friend or relative. Within the letter should be a list of the classes, schedules of classes, ages to be enrolled, costs, hours, and contact person for enrollment. Sample recruitment letters and pre-registration forms are shown in Figures 31 and 32, respectively.

COMMUNITY BULLETINS

Notices in community bulletins can also be used for recruitment, and posters can be placed in stores around the community. Flyers can also be productive, placed in residential doors or on cars in shopping center parking lots.

TELEPHONE

Advertisements in the yellow pages of the telephone book are among the best continuous forms of advertisement. When people call to inquire about enrollment, be sure to have in mind the school's philosophy and all pertinent information concerning class cost. Be courteous and pleasant on the phone; first impressions will either gain or lose that potential parent. Always be helpful and listen—it may seem silly, but if you smile at the phone while talking, it will come through to the person at the other end. Always answer the phone with joy,

---

ABC PRESCHOOL

STATE CERTIFIED PROGRAM

Ages: Three Years–Kindergarten
For Information call 555-0000

Figure 30. Sample school sign.

ABC Preschool

Parents:

I know fall is a long way off, but now is the time for our present parents to pre-register their children for primary school.

You now have the opportunity to pre-register before I open registration to the community the first of February.

Classes are as follows:

Three year olds—Mrs. Jones   Two days—$32.00
   Morning 8:00–10:45 M-W or T-TH
   Afternoon 11:30–2:15 M-W or T-TH

Younger four year olds—Mrs. Smith   Two days—$32.00
   Morning 8:00–10:45 M-W or T-TH
   Afternoon 11:30–2:15 M-W or T-TH

Regular four year olds—Mrs. Cline   Two days—$42.00
   Morning 8:00–11:00 M-W-F
   Afternoon 11:30–2:30 M-W-F
   Morning 8:00–11:00 T-TH   Two days—$32.00

Pre-Kindergarten—Mrs. Gray   Four days—$52.00
   Morning 8:00–11:00 M-T-W-TH
   Afternoon 11:30–2:30 M-T-W-TH

Kindergarten—Mrs. Stanley   Five days—$58.00
   Morning 8:00–11:00 M-T-W-TH-F

Please fill out the enclosed form indicating class preference, age of child, and teacher preference. Return to school by February 6th. If you have any questions feel free to call.

Thank you,

Director

Figure 31. Sample recruitment letter to parents.

Child's Name _____ Birth Date _____

Class Preference _____ Days _____

Time _____

Teacher _____

*An application will be sent at the end of January for you to complete and the registration fee will be due at that time. (This is just a pre-registration form, not the required application for class enrollment.)

**Your child is now enrolled in: Teacher _____
Circle one of the below:

Three Year   Younger Four   Regular Four   Pre-Kind.   Kind.

***Children will be placed by age as per application.

Figure 32. Sample pre-registration form.

stating the school's name and yours. For example: "Good morning, ABC Preschool, Mrs. Jones speaking."

Be sure to listen carefully without distractions and answer questions honestly and pleasantly. The same questions will be asked over and over again, but remember to answer as if this is the first time you have heard the question. Telephone impression is very important, for each parent that calls is primarily concerned about his/her child. You must relate concern about their children and be caring and helpful. Do not hurry a parent or act bored or unconcerned; many programs lose enrollment because of the way the phone is answered. This may seem like a trivial task, but the phone conversation between the school and a potential parent is one of the most vital points in gaining additional enrollment.

Some parents will wish to visit the school prior to actual registration. Every parent who enrolls a child should make a pre-registration visit to see the school program first-hand and talk to the director and teacher(s). This visit should be at the parents' convenience and should be a welcomed part of pre-registration activities.

WORD OF MOUTH

This form of advertisement is the best, and is also the one over which the school has the least control. People who enjoy the program will tell their friends, relatives, neighbors, etc., which provides the school with "free" advertisement. Experience has shown that newspaper advertising is not as effective as "word of mouth." If a program is good, parents will voice their satisfaction to others. However, if parents are not satisfied, they will also voice their opinions of the school. The director and staff must talk to parents, always listen to their complaints, and address their concerns in a professional and loving manner. Parents will then share with others the fact that even though they had a complaint, the preschool was willing to listen and help. A bad situation can be turned into an advantage for the school when problems are handled in a diplomatic manner. In working out complaints, do it honestly—remember, not all problems can be solved, and there will be times when parents go away angry. Accept these times for what they are, knowing that the school tried to settle them in a professional manner. Such experiences should not be viewed as failures, but as learning opportunities. If the program is of good professional quality, it will weather these little storms when they come.

There are many types of recruitment. Pick the best for the particular situation and program. Most importantly, remember that the first personal contact is the one that will be the most lasting, so make it pleasant and informative. *Smile!*

Registration

After the initial parent contact, information about the school should be sent to each parent. This information should include a thank-you for their interest, instructions on how to fill out the enclosed application, a price list of programs offered, the supply fee, the registration fee, the schedule for the start of school, and a phone number where the director can be reached if the parents have any questions. Figures 33–36 include documents that would be enclosed in such an information packet.

ABC Preschool

CLASSES AND PRICE LIST

Kindergarten—8:00–11:00 A.M. Monday–Friday
  Fees: Registration: $48.00
  Tuition: $58.00 monthly
  Supply fee: $28.00 per semester
  *Child must be five by October 1

Pre-Kindergarten—8:00–11:00 A.M. Monday–Thursday
                or 11:30–2:30 P.M. Monday–Thursday
  Fees: Registration: $28.00
  Tuition: $52.00 monthly
  Supply fee: $25.00 per semester

Regular Fours—8:00–11:00 A.M. Mon-Wed-Fri
              11:30–2:30 P.M. Mon-Wed-Thurs
              8:00–11:00 A.M. Tues-Thurs
  Fees: Registration: $20.00
  Tuition: $32.00 monthly (two days)
           $40.00 monthly (three days)
  Supply fee: $20.00 per semester (two days)
              $23.00 per semester (three days)

Younger Fours—8:00–10:45 A.M. Mon-Wed or Tues-Thurs
              11:30–2:15 P.M. Mon-Wed or Tues-Thurs
  Fees: Registration: $20.00
  Tuition: $32.00 monthly
  Supply fee: $20.00 per semester
  *Child must be four between July 1–December 31

Three Years—8:00–10.45 A.M. Mon-Wed or Tues-Thurs
            11:30–2:15 P.M. Mon-Wed or Tues-Thurs
  Fees: Registration: $20.00
  Tuition: $32.00 monthly
  Supply fee: $20.00 per semester
  *Child must be three by December 31

*Each child is required to have on record with the school, prior to the first day of school, the following:
  Birth Certificate
  Health Certificate
  Immunization Record in progress

Figure 33. Example parent information sheet.

ABC Preschool

(For Preschool Classes)

Dear Parents,

Thank you for your interest in ABC Preschool. Enclosed you will find an application. Please read all material carefully and complete entire application before returning the application to the school.

Please mark on your application the session you wish to enroll your child in. Upon receipt of the application and a registration fee of $20.00 (which is non-refundable), due when you return the application, your child will be enrolled for the fall. All classes are filled on a first-come basis; so to be assured of the session you desire, it is important that you return your application and registration fee promptly. Your cancelled check will serve as your confirmation.

Tuition and fees for the school year are as follows: (Price quotations are for each child enrolled.)

Tuition: $32.00 per month, due on or before the first of each month, beginning September 1, and ending May 1.

Supply: $20.00 per semester, due with the September and the January tuition.

Registration Fee: $20.00, due when the application is returned. This fee is nonrefundable.

School is scheduled to begin the week of August 31. There will be a parent meeting and an Open House for the children during the week of August 24th. Exact dates and times for these meetings will be sent to you around the end of July.

If you have any questions, feel free to call and discuss them. I can be contacted at school, 000-0000, Monday thru Friday, from 8 A.M. until 2:30 P.M.

See you in August,

Director

Enclosures

P.S. To enroll in this fall's session, your child must be three years old by December 31st.

Figure 34. Sample letter to prospective parents.

(For Kindergarten Classes)

Dear Parents,

Thank you for your interest in ABC Kindergarten. Enclosed you will find an application. Please read all material carefully and complete the entire application before returning.

State law requires students be five years old before October 1st. Special requests for deviation must be handled through the director on an individual basis.

Each child is required to have on record with the school, prior to the first day of school, the following:

Birth Certificate

Health Certificate

Immunization Record in progress

The curriculum is structured by the regulations set forth by the state, enabling each child to have the necessary requirements to enter first grade. The kindergarten teachers are appropriately certified.

Tuition is $58.00 per month, due on or before the first of each month, beginning September 1st and ending May 1st.

Supply fee is $28.00 per semester. The first fee is included in the registration fee, and the second is due with the January tuition.

Please complete all information on the application and return promptly, with a fee of $48.00, which is nonrefundable. This fee is for registration, and will also cover the first semester supply fee.

School is scheduled to begin the week of August 31. There will be a parent meeting and an Open House for the children during the week of August 24th. Exact dates and times for these meetings will be sent to you around the end of July.

If you have any questions, feel free to call and discuss them. I can be contacted at school, 000-0000, Monday thru Friday, from 8 A.M. until 2:30 P.M.

See you in August,

Director

Figure 35. Sample letter to prospective parents.

ABC Preschool

APPLICATION FOR ENROLLMENT
Three Year Old Class

Please return the fee with your completed application.
Registration Fee: $20.00 NONREFUNDABLE

PLEASE CIRCLE CLASS DESIRED:

Morning (8:00–11:45): Mon-Wed or Tues-Thurs

Afternoon (11:30–2:15): Mon-Wed or Tues-Thurs

Child's Name: _____
(Last)   (First)   (Middle)

Birth Date: _____
Home Phone: _____
Address: _____
(Street)   (City)

_____
(State)   (Zip Code)

Father's Name: _____
Place of Employment: _____
Work Phone: _____

Mother's Name: _____
Place of Employment: _____
Work Phone: _____

Child's Physician: _____ Phone: _____
Allergies: _____

Church: _____

My child uses which hand? Right _____   Left _____
Fears: _____
Names of other children: _____

Parents' Signature: _____
Date: _____

(Please add any further information that you feel would aid your
child's teacher on the back of this application.)

Figure 36. Sample enrollment application.

The registration form shown as Figure 36 was designed for the three year olds; other classes and age groups can easily use the same basic form by changing just the pertinent information. The registration application should state the name of the school, age of child, what the application is for, registration fee—refundable or nonrefundable, classes—days and times offered, information about the child, information about parent (requesting parents' place of employment is very helpful if an emergency arises and the parent needs to be contacted), child's physician and phone number, allergies, fears, hand that the child uses, previous preschool experience, names and ages of siblings, and lastly the parents' signatures and date of application. Space should be provided on the back of the application for parents' comments concerning their child. Other items may need to be added, but a word of caution—do not make the application too much longer. Some schools ask for marital status of parents, but it is not necessary to do so because most parents will include that information with the parent information section, or in their comments.

When classes become filled, mark through those sections and write *full*, so parents will know what choices they have left.

Upon receipt of application and registration fee the child's name, date of entry, and fee collected should be entered in a ledger under the class choice. This provides an ongoing class list, which will show how classes are filling and help adjust the total numbers for the preschool. The application should immediately be filed in a folder for that class. If an organized file and ledger are kept, it will avoid confusion. Remember, many parents will want to switch their child's classes to suit their schedules. When this begins, applications must be organized or there will be much confusion as to what classes are filled. Always record everything—first enrollment, changes, payment, etc.—this will be a lifesaver later.

At the first staff meeting, each teacher should be given the application form of each child in his/her classroom, in order to have pertinent information about the child at his/her fingertips. Remind staff that these application forms are confidential and should be stored as such. A copy should be made for the director to keep in the office records.

The week of parent orientation will be wild with changes in classes, payment of fees, etc. Be ready for this by doing accurate recording during registration. Parent orientation will be discussed in detail later.

MULTIPLE CHILDREN REGISTRATION

Some schools have a policy not to give a cost break to parents who have more than one child enrolled. All fees are the same for each child enrolled, so if a parent has two children in a two-day, four-year-old class, the fees are regular fees—registration fee is $20.00 per child, supply fee is $20.00 per semester per child, and tuition is $32.00 per month per child. This policy sometimes is hard to enforce, but remember—if the school is nonprofit and self-supporting, this policy is the only way the program can be maintained.

EXCEPTION

There may be times when exceptions to the collection of fees would be appropriate. Some schools offer scholarships or reduced fees. These circumstances should be handled on an individual basis and kept confidential. Be sure when offering reduced or paid fees to discuss with the parents their financial status. Most parents in financial trouble are reluctant to take a handout, so discuss reduced (reasonable) fees for them at the appropriate time. Remember, the preschool is a service to the community and should reach out to those in need. Do not deprive a child because of finances, but do not overload the program with free or reduced-fee children, or the program will suffer. The school is walking a fine line in this area (as we all do), but concern for children must be weighted with concern for the program's stability. There may be times in the middle of the year when financial problems hit parents. Even if the parents pay only $5.00 a month, they are trying, and many times when their problems end they will catch up on what they did not pay. This does not always happen; don't be surprised if the preschool never gets paid. Remember, it is the child we want to help, and that is a portion of our reward and service to the community. However, the preschool should not be seen or perceived as a "public" or free school.

A final note is that children of staff members should attend free—it is one of the benefits the staff receives.

LATE REGISTRATION

During the first three weeks of school, many parents call to register their children (for example, older siblings are going to school, and they now want a younger child to go). These parents should be charged the same fees for these children as all other students. Many times there will be parents that balk at this, but stand firm. They should have no special privileges. Remember, it was the parent who was late enrolling the student, not the preschool. Be tactful, careful, and listen, but stand firm on the fees.

In the months following the start-up of school there may be one or two new enrollees each month. The registration fee is the same, supply fee prorated, and the tuition is the same each month. Some schools do not take new children after March 15, because it is difficult for the child to make friends in such a short time. An exception to this rule would be for families moving to town with children who have been actively involved in a previous preschool program in another location.

DROPOUTS

Expect some children not to show up for the first day of school. Some parents will call and withdraw their children, other parents will have to be called to confirm the withdrawal of their children. On the night of parent orientation for each class, a parent not attending (call each child's name from the application at the meeting) should be telephoned that night to ascertain if they have changed plans. If not, then immediately inform parents that their space in the class will be filled. This method works very well, eliminating the need to hold an unwanted space and taking the guesswork out of class size.

Some parents will start children and then pull them out of school. Their registration fees are never refundable, and tuition for that month and supply fee for that semester must be prorated for refund. Make these financial details very clear "up front" with parents to avoid unneeded problems. Remember, the preschool is a business and all matters must be dealt with in a business-like manner. Try to avoid "hard feelings" when possible, because word of mouth will be the greatest asset or detriment, as previously stated.

Parent Permission Forms

Parent permission forms are extremely important and must be on file for each child. These forms should be given to the teacher to file with the child's application when they are completed. Require that these forms be completed, signed, and dated prior to a child's first day of attendance in school. These forms can be distributed the night of parent orientation and should be due back the day of the child's open house. If a parent does not attend orientation or open house, then the form should be read and signed prior to the child's entrance in school. This may seem strict, but without this form the school cannot take action if a child is hurt, etc. This form is designed to provide the school with necessary information, and every child enrolled must have a completed form to remain in school. Legal counsel may be required when designing the form. Figure 37 is a sample parent permission form that has been used, and which was developed by an attorney.

The parent permission form covers use of equipment, activities, walks, field trips, evaluations, pictures, emergency procedures and contacts (this is why parents are asked on the application for place of employment and work phone numbers), payment of incurred expenses, and waiver of responsibility for false information on application form. Separate forms for the required information can be used, but each one must be kept on file with the child's application. Some schools keep an emergency form only, but send a field trip form such as the one in Figure 38 each time they take a field trip.

Experience has shown it works well to keep the parent permission form on file and notify parents prior to taking a field trip—stating destination, date, time, and name of teacher. This procedure is much easier, and since permission was given at the beginning of school, all children are assured of going (rather than tracking down a parent on the day of the trip

I hereby grant permission for my child to use all the play equipment and participate in all of the activities of the school.

I hereby grant permission for my child to leave the school premises under the supervision of a staff member for neighborhood walks or for field trips in an authorized vehicle.

I hereby grant permission for my child to be included in evaluations and pictures connected with the school program.

I hereby grant permission for the director or acting director to take whatever steps are necessary, which may include, but are not limited to, the following:

(1) Attempt to contact a parent or guardian.
(2) Attempt to contact parent or guardian through any of the persons listed below.*
(3) Attempt to contact the child's physician.
(4) If we cannot contact you or your child's physician, we will do any or all of the following:
  a. call another physician or paramedics
  b. call an ambulance
  c. have the child taken to an emergency hospital in the company of a staff member
(5) Any expenses incurred under #4, above, will be borne by the child's family.
(6) The school will not be responsible for anything that may happen as a result of false information given at the time of enrollment.

*Persons to contact in case of emergency (other than parent):
1st Name: _____ Phone # _____
2nd Name: _____ Phone # _____
3rd Name: _____ Phone # _____

Signed: _____ Date: _____
              Parent or Legal Guardian

Figure 37. Sample parent permission form.

because of a forgotten permission note). Since permission forms are an essential legal part of the program, give great care and consideration to the form that is going to be used and update it when necessary.

Handbook of Parent Information

The school's parent handbook should be visually appealing and informative. Everything that the parents need to know should be included, but only the most pertinent information should be stated. The handbook should be a guide, not a detailed rules and regulations book. Every area of concern should be addressed.

Appendix A is a sample of an entire handbook as a guide for consideration. Included with the handbook is a class information sheet, which is given to parents at their parent orientation meeting. This class sheet gives the teacher's name, the teacher's home phone number (some may not want to be included since phone numbers can cause a problem for the privacy of the teachers), and other pertinent information. Look over both of these information sheets—each program needs to develop its own handbook, which includes its own specific areas of concern.

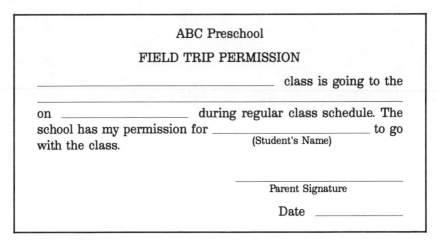

Figure 38. Sample field trip permission form.

Child's Identification Card

The child's identification card is for the protection of the children. Each child is given a number or a letter of the alphabet printed on a $5'' \times 7''$ card, which parents place in the passenger's side windshield of their car. A corresponding list of children by classes is posted inside the school. When a parent arrives to pick up his/her child, the number in the car is matched in the school. This procedure insures that the person picking up the child has authorization from the parents to do so. If a car does not display a card, then the child is not released (even if it is the parent). This is sometimes frustrating to drivers, but it does insure the child's safety from unauthorized persons, and also protects the school from a lawsuit that could ensue by releasing a child to the wrong person.

The procedure will also quicken the loading procedure. The staff can rotate schedules in loading and unloading children from parents' cars. When the staff loads children in and out of cars, the problem of parents having to park their cars to bring children to the room can be alleviated.

Using child identification cards also gives the parents' authority to other persons they designate to pick up their children. If parents are in a car pool, need a baby-sitter to pick up the child, or have other persons to pick up their children, they simply provide the card (or make another one with their child's I.D. number on it). The person picking up the child shows the staff the I.D. card, and the child will be released to them. In such instances, parents should inform the staff that they are having someone else pick up the child so the school can let the child know. This procedure is for the protection of both the school and the child. Remember, if you use this procedure or any other, explain the method on the night of Parent Orientation. This way parents are familiar with the method, and have a chance to ask any questions they may have. The most important rule for loading and unloading children is this—safety!

Parents' cars line up along the street and pull up to the sidewalk where the staff are waiting to open the car door and greet both parent and child. Children enter the building (while other staff members supervise) and go to their respective

ARRIVAL

Parents *please* do not park and get out of your car. Doors open five minutes prior to the start of class (according to school clocks). Please remain in your car until the doors open. The children will be unloaded from the cars by the teachers. After your child has been unloaded, please exit on the street.

Figure 39. Sample arrival policy.

classrooms. Sample arrival and departure policies are shown in Figures 39 and 40, respectively.

Teacher Orientation

Staff members should be notified about future employment prior to the closing of a school year or by letter prior to the first staff meeting. A sample orientation letter is shown in Figure 41. At this first staff meeting all teachers and assistants should be present.

At any staff meeting refreshments should be available. A potluck lunch, or dinner or snacks provided by the school can help provide a more relaxed atmosphere. At this, as at all staff meetings, the director needs to conduct business and work-

DEPARTURE

Parents PLEASE do not park and get out of your car. Children will be loaded into cars by the teachers. *Parents must have their child's identification number* inside the passenger side windshield in order to pick up their child. If you do not have the identification number, you will not receive your child. This rule applies to everyone and will be strictly enforced for your child's safety. After your child has been loaded, please exit onto _____ street.

Figure 40. Sample departure policy.

ABC Preschool

Dear Staff,

I hope you are enjoying a beautiful summer vacation. First, our staff meeting has been scheduled for Thursday, August _____ at 10:00 A.M. At this meeting, will you please have your supply list ready for me, so I can get it totalled and sent in by the 17th. The amount to figure for this first supply list is $125.00. There will be another staff meeting on Monday, August _____. This meeting will be when you get your class registration/application sheets, finalize school calendar information, and receive information to include in materials you give the parents at Orientation.

I will be at work every day beginning August 3rd from 9:00 A.M. to 12:00 noon. If you want to come and work on your rooms, that will be fine, but you are not required to be here.

See you on Thursday, August _____ at 10:00 A.M.!

Sincerely,

The Director

Figure 41. Sample staff orientation letter.

ABC Preschool

AGENDA FOR AUGUST 15, 19

(1) Welcome
(2) Introduction to staff
(3) Distribution of applications and materials to assigned staff
(4) Clarification and discussion on application information
(5) Appointment of parent and child orientation schedules
(6) Discussion and clarification policies (old and new) of school
(7) Ordering of supplies for school year
(8) In-service programs (discussed under "Staffing")
(9) Other concerns of staff
(10) Dismissal
(11) Refreshments
(12) Work in rooms in preparation for opening of school

Figure 42. Sample staff meeting agenda.

shops (teacher in-service training) to assist staff in becoming acquainted with new policies, educational, or professional programs, and having the opportunity to discuss concerns.

Staff meetings should be conducted in a relaxed but informative atmosphere. A close staff will help each other in many ways. There should be a comradeship within the staff, so they can share problems and joys, and ask each other for advice. A staff that works together can demonstrate to parents the concern that the school has for a child. Not all staff members will work together in harmony, but one of the duties of the director is to keep the staff pointed in the best direction for the common good of the school. This will be discussed in further detail in the "Staffing" chapter.

The initial staff meetings should be used to pull the staff together for the coming year. The agenda should be written and distributed to the staff before the actual meeting. One possible agenda is shown in Figure 42.

The staff meeting will require time, so allow at least two hours of uninterrupted time to get all items completed and to permit discussion. Remember, any discussion of information on the student applications is *confidential*, and should never be repeated outside the staff meeting. This is a rule that must never be broken. The initial staff meeting needs to have some time that is relaxing; it should be informal, but organized. Any staff information forms or other forms should be completed by staff at this time. Staff should also be allowed ample time to prepare their room for parent orientation, plus time to prepare the packets of material to be passed out on the evening of parent orientation.

Parent Orientation

About three weeks prior to the opening of school a letter of welcome should be sent to parents of enrolled children. This letter states the time and date of the orientation meeting, as shown in Figure 43.

Depending on the size of the program, more than one parent orientation meeting may be needed. With a program of 250 children, at least five separate meetings are recommended.

Dear Parents,

Welcome!! Summer is drawing to a close and it's time to think and plan for the coming school year. I am anxiously awaiting the opportunity to meet you and your child, so we can share many experiences with you.

Please mark the following date on your calendar, and plan to attend: _____

The Parent Orientation Meeting will be in the Educational Building at 7:00 P.M. This meeting is for *parents* only!!! The Children's Open House will be held _____.

The exact time of your child's Open House will be given at the Parent Orientation Meeting.

As always, feel free to contact me at any time. We hope to see you at the Parent Orientation Meeting.

Sincerely,

Director

Figure 43. Sample parent orientation letter.

These meetings should last no longer than an hour and need to be in the evening when both parents can attend.

The format of the meeting works well using the agenda outlined in Figure 44, which should be presented by the director of the school.

The parent orientation procedure also determines which parents are not present, and will enable the director to contact them later to determine whether their children are attending or have withdrawn. This procedure is done by class time and days (Monday–Wednesday, 8–11 A.M.) to insure the correct placement of the child. Many parents enroll five to eight months prior to the opening of school and forget the time and days for which they enrolled their child. Some parents will want to change classes to correspond with new car pools, work schedules, baby-sitters, etc., so *be prepared!*

Parent orientation meetings will be the most exhausting time of year, so get plenty of rest! These first impressions will be the most lasting for parents. Keep your cool and be pleasant. Many parents are new at this experience, so a calm presentation will help reassure them.

If fees are being collected at the parent orientation meeting, records should be prepared in advance. Write receipts for cash, and take time to mark down each payment immediately. The parent meeting will be an evening of meeting many new parents and giving out a lot of information. Not taking time to record payments could easily result in forgetting where money came from. Give parents ample time at these meetings to ask questions—in fact, encourage these questions. Parents need to understand that the people in the program have a genuine concern and love for their children. These meetings take time and energy, but are one of the best public relations mediums that the school can use.

Most of all, the director should be available to assist or discuss any concerns with parents. The director's availability and time are most important. Parents are depending on the preschool for the care of their children, and this evening can help

---

ABC Preschool

AGENDA FOR FALL 1990 MEETINGS

(1) Welcome

(2) Opening

(3) Introductions of teacher and assistant

(4) *Roll call of children

(5) Discussion of material
   a. Handbook, class information sheet, permission sheet, etc.
   b. Collection of fees

(6) Teacher will discuss curriculum used and the skills to be taught

(7) Question and answer time

(8) Dismissal to see classrooms and meet teachers

*When the director calls each child's name from the class roster the staff gives that parent a packet that contains: handbook, class information sheet, parent permission form, child's I.D. card, car pool sheet, skill sheet from teacher, and other information that the teacher wants the parents to receive.

Figure 44. Sample parent orientation meeting agenda.

establish a trust for the program and staff of the preschool. For most parents this will be their first experience at being separated from their child. They need to feel confident with all aspects of the program, and to understand that they are always welcome to discuss their concerns, fears, etc., with the director and/or staff. Actions will let parents know that the staff is reaching out to them. It doesn't have to be said, but remember—"actions speak louder than words."

Child Orientation

Time must be set aside for the child's orientation to school; each child should be scheduled for orientation. Experience has found this is best done by classes. On the morning following the parent orientation, children should be scheduled to come to school to meet the teacher, aide, and other children in their class. An example would be: children in the three-year-olds (Monday–Wednesday) class would come from 8:30–9:00 A.M. (It is best to allow only half an hour). This gives the child time to see the room and what's in it; to meet the staff and other children; to see the unloading and loading area; and to get the general feel for this new experience. This short time will not alleviate the crying that is associated with the first day of school, but it does minimize the fear of being in a new place without parents.

Child orientation lets children know that parents approve of the school, and that the school is a safe place to be. Parents are to accompany children to these orientation sessions and remain with them for the orientation. This will reinforce the child's positive feelings toward the school experience.

During this orientation, it is suggested that parents show their children where and how they will load and unload from the car. They need to "walk through" the procedure with their child. This will give children an idea of how the first day of school will be.

All children enrolled in the school should attend orientation. This is an important part of the school experience, and the director should impress on parents the importance of their attendance.

Always imagine yourself in this first situation. Many children will experience feelings of fear, remorse, and abandonment. The most important thing that can be done for children during these first few days is to reassure them that their parents will return. Holding them, loving them, and keeping them busy will make the time pass faster.

Changes in Class Assignment

During the first three weeks of school there will be changes in the class assignments. These will come from new applications, withdrawals, and changes made between classes. Staff should be notified of these changes immediately. The director needs to be mindful of the placement of children. Do not overload classes; try to assign children evenly across the board. Staff gripes come easily when one teacher is overloaded and another is underfilled. The size of classes should be watched closely by the director.

Some children will need to be moved within classes because of new parent schedules, baby-sitters, or inappropriate parent placement of the child. Work with the staff and parents before moving the child; doing this will let everyone know the reasons and purposes of the move. Always allow staff to take part in changes of child assignment. They will know where the child fits best, and it allows them to be a part of the decision.

Car Pools

Many parents will need help in finding car pools. The school can maintain and supply phone numbers of other parents in the area of residence of the parent that is looking for a car pool. It is then the parent's responsibility to secure the car pool. Do not suggest contacting parents to form car pools. (Within the sample handbook contained in Appendix A is a section on car pools. It is a good idea to include similar information in each parent handbook, and to ask parents to read this section carefully.) Personnel need to know pertinent information concerning the children that do ride in car pools for loading purposes. A sample information sheet is shown in Figure 45.

Staff should not be permitted to drive children to and from school; liability insurance does not cover this. Car pools can be great, or they can be a headache. Parents need to be responsible for the car pooling; it is not the school's responsibility.

Class Roster Sheets

Teachers should be provided with a plan book so that they can keep their class rosters at hand. Rosters help the teachers keep track of absenteeism, etc. Roster sheets can be created, but they should be kept within the teacher's plan book.

ABC Preschool

PLEASE READ CAREFULLY

Dear Parents,

If you are in a car pool, please fill out the information below and leave it with your child's teacher.

Your child's identification card will be determined by this information.

Children in Car Pool	Class	Days
(1)		
(2)		
(3)		
(4)		
(5)		

Thank you for your help. You will receive your child's identification card at the Open House.

Sincerely,

Director

Figure 45. Sample car pool information sheet.

It is the policy of ABC School Board that any parents who are consistently tardy in the pickup of their child (consistent tardiness means more than three late violations without phoning, or more than five violations with phoning) will, after the third violation, be informed of the following steps, which will be enforced:

(1) Upon the next late violation, a charge of $5.00 for every five, or part of five minutes that a parent is past class dismissal time.

(2) Payment for the late fee will be made the day of the violation at the time of loading of the child.

(3) Failure to pay the late charge or failure to pick up child on time will result in the child's immediate withdrawal from ABC Preschool.

ABC School Board regrets the necessity of having to take such action, but because of some parents' repeated tardiness, no other choice remains.

It is the parent's responsibility to be in line five minutes prior to the release of their child's class. It is also their responsibility to call the school to inform the director if they are having problems and will be late in picking up their child.

Times for pickup were given at each parent meeting at the beginning of the school year. Parents were informed of these times and are expected to abide by them.

Figure 46. Sample school board policy for late pickup of children.

Waiting Lists

Waiting lists should be maintained by the director if the classes are full. Before placing a child on a waiting list, the director should try to enroll the child in another suitable class that has an opening.

Some schools keep waiting lists a year or two ahead, but this is not recommended because of bookkeeping. "Years to Come" lists may be kept, but it is much simpler to request parents to call in January (prior to the next school year) requesting information for the upcoming year. Each school must determine its individual policy on waiting lists.

Policy of Late Pickup of Children

Parents need to be made aware of the school policy at orientation. A copy needs to be included with their packet, and the director should make the parents aware of its contents. Figure 46 is an example that can be used for orientation.

This is a delicate matter, and must be handled professionally. Remember, it is the child that suffers most. Remind parents of that fact, and their responsibilities to the child and the school staff. Be tactful, but abide by the policies of the school board.

CHAPTER SEVEN

Curriculum

> CHILDREN HAVE NEVER BEEN VERY GOOD
> AT LISTENING TO THEIR ELDERS, BUT
> THEY HAVE NEVER FAILED TO IMITATE THEM.
>
> —James Baldwin

WITHIN the preschool educational program, the school board, director, and staff should develop school practices appropriate to the educational functions of children. All concerned with the program should remember that early childhood education is very unlike elementary school.

Children of this age are explorers, discoverers, and imaginers. They are searching and experimenting with a new world each day. The duty of early childhood educators is to provide the atmosphere and opportunities for a child to explore the new world, while building a sense of self-worth and self-confidence. The methods used should not include a student desk, but rather tables and floor space, so that a child can feel, smell, manipulate, and explore. Creativity and imagination must be encouraged. Dittos have limited value in this setting. Children must experience their surroundings and must have ample freedom to choose. This is a child's world, sensed through a child's experiences. Do not make it adult-level, or even on the level of a kindergarten child.

Curriculum for early childhood programs should be determined by what's worth knowing for the young child. The teacher, in choosing what to teach, is performing one of the most vital tasks and is making a statement about goals, values, and what the teacher knows about young children. In determining the basis for development of curriculum, the question arises, "What is worth knowing?" The young child needs to know how to take care of himself/herself; the child needs to know about himself/herself, as well as about others, their cultures, and the world he/she lives in; and the child should appreciate and understand his/her physical and social environment. Thus, the basis for the curriculum for the young child is competence, knowledge, appreciation, and caring for oneself, the world, and other people.

Early childhood education is "humanistic," and it operates in an atmosphere where a child is allowed to be a child. The child is allowed to learn by doing, and is loved and nurtured for trying whether he/she fails or accomplishes the task at hand. The environment of the classroom should be risk-free because the child initiates the learning. Play, "the child's work," is his/her means to explore and discover his/her environment in a safe and controlled climate. The curriculum should be formed around the seven basic material areas: natural play, active play, constructive toys, manipulative toys, dramatic play, art, and books and records. These are included to develop a "soft" learning environment for the child to learn and grow in risk-free.

Types of Curriculum

The development of children falls into four areas (social, intellectual, physical, and emotional) providing teachers with categories on which to build learning experiences that foster growth and development. Although within the four areas age and developmental levels differ, the framework upon which the process is formed guides the child through the curriculum to assist in mastery of given skills at each level. Children are guided by the teacher through this process by identification of goals and objectives; designing of activities and experiences; and observing and assessing children for mastery of skills. Appropriate skills lists for young children have been compiled by the National Association of Educators of Young Children to provide the teacher with a guideline for a developmentally appropriate curriculum. This guideline should be used to form the curriculum enabling children to follow the nationally accepted developmental framework. The following discussion of the individual areas of curriculum use the national guidelines as their basis.

Intellectual Curriculum

This area of curriculum deals with the logical development of a child by taking past experiences and applying them to new ones. This curriculum is taught through the use of the inquiry process. Divided into six steps for learning through discovery, the process allows the child opportunities to explore his/her environment and to learn through his/her own experiences in developing the following concepts:

- *Exploring:* allows the child to use his/her senses to observe, investigate, and manipulate the environment.
- *Identifying:* provides the opportunity for naming and describing what he/she experiences.
- *Classifying:* provides grouping of objects or experiences by their common properties.
- *Comparing/Contrasting:* allows observation of similarities and differences between objects or experiences.
- *Hypothesizing:* uses data from past experiences to make guesses about what might happen.
- *Generalizing:* applies previous experiences to new events.

This process produces new ideas and creates an environment for discovery, and a new way of thinking. This gives the child time to explore, and should be guided by the teacher using open questioning.

The four functional areas of this curriculum include:

- Math
- Science
- Social Studies
- Health

MATH

Building on the work of Piaget and Dewey, the traditional concepts of what young children can learn has led to a rethinking of the math curriculum. Math for young children needs to help them develop a sense of their physical and social world. Math experiences form ideas and a framework from which the child can build concepts of numbers and number relationships, interact with other children and adults, develop language, take time to reflect and think about experiences encountered, and provide opportunities where adults can guide a child's thinking and understanding of their environment and its relationship to math concepts.

Young children learn more than counting and sorting within a math curriculum. They also need to know the concepts of:

(1) *Classification*—Children develop the concept of classification by learning to understand that they can group objects together by size, shape, color, etc. They need to be able to perceive similarities and differences, and understand the concept of sets. Sorting and grouping objects are important skills that are developed for use in later math functions.

(2) *Space*—Children develop the concept of space by learning to understand the relationships of objects based on location, direction, and distance. They further develop this concept by placing toys on shelves and realizing position of items on the shelf. In play, they experience concepts of far/near, left/right, up/down, which provide relationships to position the self within the environment.

(3) *Numbers*—Children develop the concept of numbers by comparing sets, position, quantity, and one-to-one correspondence. The understanding of what makes 2, 3, 4, and in what order numbers exist. They develop concepts of more, less, or the same and begin to understand number position. Teachers can develop one-to-one correspondence in many ways throughout the day by using counters, rods, cups at snack time, and carpet squares during circle time.

(4) *Measurement*—Children develop the concept of measurement by comparing quantities, size, weight, or volume against a standard. For example, how many cups fill a water table? How many blocks long is a table? How many beads fill a cup?

(5) *Seriation*—Children develop the concept of ordering

(arranging objects in sequence based on differences in size, texture, color, and weight) by being allowed the opportunity to explore such relationships as shortest/ tallest, largest/smallest, brightest/dullest, etc. Growth charts provide a comparison of children's sizes. Teachers can make a growth graph of children's height to develop the concept of graphing.

(6) *Time*–Children develop the concept of time, the sequencing of events in daily life, by the routine in such activities as: snack time, lunch, nap, outdoor play, etc. Children also begin to understand length of time (duration) in relation to length of activities within their environment.

When developing the curriculum, teachers need to provide opportunities that foster the child's ability to: count; recognize numbers, groups, and quantities; select groups and sets; recognize number symbols; graph; use ordinals; compare size and amount; understand time and time relationships; and perform simple operations.

The teaching of this curriculum must provide activities that enrich the environment of the child and provide interaction with others. Math activities occur throughout the daily program and should not be limited to interest centers or planned group activities. A child learns math throughout his/her daily life and routines. Teachers need to incorporate math into all areas of their curriculum planning, providing opportunities to use and develop these concepts.

SCIENCE

In this curriculum area, the teacher's main purpose is to encourage the natural curiosity of the child, while establishing relationships to other curriculum areas. Science uses the child's exploring instincts to discover the world he/she lives in, and to acquire an identity of himself/herself as a functioning part of that world. Science can be divided into physical and life sciences. Life science includes the biological, physiological, and ecological functions of a child's life.

Life Science

Children want to know more about themselves—where they come from, how they live, and how life exists around them. They are curious about life around them and how it survives. Because of this interest and curiosity, life sciences are included in the curriculum.

(1) *Biology*, which can be defined as the study of animals, and *botany*, which can be defined as the study of the growth, structure, and origin of plants, are important areas to be included. Children explore their environment and assume anything that moves is alive. Because children learn by acting on objects, concepts of natural phenomena must be developed through manipulation of items within the children's environment. Watching living things grow and change aid in the exploration of that environment. The use of living animals and plants (birds, fish, trees, etc.) helps children discover the relationship of life to their own existence.

(2) *Physiology* can be defined as the study of processes and functions of living organisms. Children want to know how their bodies function and grow. They are fascinated with themselves and their similarities and differences from others. Through this desire to know, a teacher can expand the curriculum to include this science and its study in many areas.

(3) *Ecology* can be defined as the study of the interaction between organisms and their environment. With today's throwaway society, children need to develop an understanding of what consequences their actions have on the existence of a safe, viable environment. Teachers can provide opportunities for children to explore and discover ways to protect and clean the world around them to ensure their future on planet Earth.

The study of the life sciences should include the child's discovery of: who they are; what they look like, and why; what lives in the world with them; and how they interact with all living things.

Physical Science

This area of science includes the physical, chemical, and geological world that a child lives in. Why and how something moves, what changes the ingredients in cooking to make cookies, and what forms our earth, are some of the topics that can be interesting to young children.

(1) *Physics* is the study of matter, form, and change. Children learn about physics when they play. On the playground, the action of the see-saw, swing, and slide provide insight into energy. They realize if dropped, things fall, and building blocks can collapse if built too high. This natural play gives them a basis for interaction with physical phenomena.

(2) *Chemistry* is the study of composition properties and transformations of organic and inorganic substances. As complicated as chemistry sounds within the context of early childhood, the simple task of cooking or watching ice change to water then steam are excellent ways to demonstrate the chemical world to children.

(3) *Geology* is the study of the formation of the earth. This can easily be incorporated within the curriculum. Rocks from a driveway, digging into the earth, visiting a museum, and talking about lakes, rivers, and streams are all ways to develop geological concepts for the children.

(4) *Astronomy* is the study of the universe beyond the earth's atmosphere. Children can observe the sun, moon, and stars and learn about the cycles of our universe. They can be exposed by television and books to the space age and its importance to our society.

The science curriculum lets the child observe, identify properties, discover relationships, and search for answers through his/her natural curiosity and desire to explore. Although many teachers feel they have inadequate skills in science, it is important to remember that young children need science to discover their world. The simple, natural scientific phenomena surrounding us are the best science curriculum a teacher could develop.

SOCIAL STUDIES

The curriculum of social studies is very broad and can be studied in diverse ways. Approaching social studies from the child's view gives him/her a knowledge based on personal experiences. The organizing framework for social studies is developed around six organizing questions that are used to relate social science fields and the appropriate concepts for young children:

1. *Who am I as a person with feelings?*

   Children learn that all people have feelings and that accepting and dealing with feelings in constructive ways benefits their life.

2. *Who am I as a member of a family?*

   Children learn that everyone is a member of a family, but that not all families are the same. They discover family similarities and what constitutes the family.

3. *Who am I as a member of a community?*

   Children learn what a community is, as well as its makeup. They discover what, how, and who makes a community function, they also learn their place within the structure.

4. *Who am I as a person from a culture?*

   Young children need to know about their culture. Through this question the teacher is prepared to discuss the varying cultures within the classroom and to assist children in discovering not only their cultural heritage but also the cultures of others.

5. *Who am I as a person in a place?*

   Children need to gain knowledge of the places in which they live and play. Teachers can provide experiences for children to discover where they live, and the qualities of these places.

6. *Who am I as a person in time?*

   Children gain knowledge by observing and experiencing time. By watching plants grow, seasons change, etc., children gain an understanding of past, present, and future.

"Who am I?" is a basis for all social studies units, whether talking about the child, family, community, or world. By developing relationships of self to others, children will discover growth in the society in which they live.

HEALTH

The health curriculum should include areas concerning: personal hygiene, self-esteem, nutrition, prevention of disease, and safety.

(1) *Personal hygiene*—Children can learn personal hygiene techniques: brushing teeth; washing hands, face, etc. This trait should be modeled by the teacher and reinforced daily.

(2) *Self-esteem*—Teachers have a responsibility to build a positive self-esteem in children. Praise, love, positive discipline techniques, and a risk-free environment promoted through a caring, nurturing, loving staff are a must for children to develop a positive self-image.

(3) *Nutrition*—Nutrition for young children is an important part of the health curriculum. Children need to be knowledgeable of choices of food and their nutritional content. The preparation of food for snacks provides excellent opportunities to present the nutrition curriculum.

(4) *Prevention of disease*—This area of the health curriculum is treated not as a planned lesson, but as a facet of personal hygiene, although the teacher should make children aware of the ways to prevent spreading diseases.

(5) *Safety*—This area is of particular concern for young children. The teacher needs to include safety of all forms within the curriculum plans. Children this age are natural explorers and fear very little. For this reason, safety discussions and practices must be included within the school program.

Materials used within the health curriculum should be appropriate to the age and the developmental level of the child.

The teacher must choose material that has been developed for the young child and present the material in a way that the young child can perceive and understand. Do not overwhelm the young child with too much in-depth material. The uses of tasting, cooking, literature, songs, painting, dancing, etc., are excellent forms for teaching the health curriculum.

Communication Curriculum

A child needs to develop social worth by discovering that he/she is an integral part of the lives of those with whom he/she comes into contact in daily life. They must be allowed the freedom to communicate with their classmates and teachers. Children must feel that their communication is valued and listened to. They must be given the opportunity to express their feelings and explore their emotions. This curriculum area is divided into language development, literature, and pre-reading/writing. No matter how divided, the communication curriculum will be the major focus of the program, and the child must be free to develop the skills within the program area.

LANGUAGE DEVELOPMENT

The development of verbal language helps children learn listening and speaking skills by communicating without formal instruction. There are several theories concerning the development of language which influence the preparation of the early childhood curriculum. The theory used here is a combination of all the theories. Educators typically believe that children develop language in various ways: through "significant others" modeling language; through developmental stages of logical thought, judgement, and reasoning; through parental influences; and so on.

The teacher has many opportunities for teaching language to the young child. The development of a language-rich environment could include the following: labeling items in the room; allowing children to participate in classroom language; asking open-ended questions; planning experiences that involve and motivate language; allowing conversation; providing opportunities for role playing and comfortable areas to talk; using fingerplays, puppet theaters, props, language games, flannelboards, books, circle time, show-n-tell, and art work; conducting field trips; and having daily music, movement, and meetings.

PRE-READING AND PRE-WRITING

Reading is the tool to unlock ideas, adventures, and relationships. The reading curriculum should provide readiness skills that include: large and small motor skills, visual and auditory discrimination, problem solving, sequencing ability, left-to-right orientation, and sensory and motor development. The goals for the pre-reading curriculum are interest in reading, knowledge of the relationship of speech to print, development of sight words, recognition of letter names, and maintenance of a print-rich environment. The teacher is responsible for providing a developmentally appropriate curriculum that includes the above. The daily student program should include labeling of items in the room, language experiences, story charts, written speech, sight vocabulary, and reading to the children. Early childhood educators favor language experience instruction as a way to introduce young children to reading. This approach uses the child's own experience to enhance his/her reading skills.

WRITING

Before children can learn to write, the development of small muscle coordination must occur. A child must develop six skills before he/she can write: small muscle coordination, eye-hand coordination, holding a writing tool, basic strokes, letter perception, and orientation to printed language. The teacher must develop a curriculum conducive to the development of the above skills before children are encouraged to write. Therefore handwriting must be developed as a part of the entire language curriculum and not as a separate curriculum.

LITERATURE

Children's experiences with literature should be enjoyable, for children who love books eventually come to love reading. Literature should be carefully chosen, and should provide a varied selection for children to gain experience and knowledge. Teachers should: design a space for individual and group reading, read with skill and responsiveness, provide experiences to expand literature, use literature as a part of the daily program, use flannelboards and puppets for presentations, use recorded stories and poems, and assist parents in the use and choosing of good literature for children. Throughout this area of the language curriculum, literature should be chosen for the child's enjoyment.

Physical Education

This area of early childhood curriculum is designed to develop both physical and sensory experiences. A child needs to use both large (gross) and small (fine) muscles in preparation for formal education. Children need to know the feel, taste, sight, and sound of their world. They need to be allowed to run, jump, climb, skip, hop, balance, walk, draw, paint, and cut. Muscles will develop in stages and teachers must be familiar with the sequences of development in order to provide appropriate activities for each child to move at his/her own rate and style through each stage. If finger muscles are not developed for cutting, the child will be incapable of cutting. Teachers must be patient and aware of the developmental stage of each child.

Creative Curriculum

The teacher's purpose in creative curriculum is to provide an environment, materials, experiences, and relationships that support creative development within a child. All children are creative in their own way, and teachers of young children must provide opportunities and an atmosphere that encourages children to experience creative abilities. This curriculum includes: art, music, drama, and movement.

ART

Art is basic to early childhood education programs and provides opportunities for children to explore and manipulate materials, and express their feelings and understanding of the world. The purpose of art is to enhance the enjoyment and satisfaction (never judge) in the social, academic, and visual symbols that are art.

The teacher should allow the child freedom in the production of art. It is the process, not the product of art, that enhances the young child. The goals of the teacher for introducing art to the young child are: making art, looking at art, evaluating art, providing a secure, risk-free environment, freedom of choice, ample time for the child to complete, and limited use of teacher patterns. The strategies for teaching art are: integrate art as a daily part of the program, discuss the activity prior to doing, let children label their work, give sincere praise of the child's work, offer minimal teacher input, discuss artwork, display objects, and develop an appreciation of the work of others. Materials used for art include: paint, printing, drawing, collage, woodworking, modeling, sewing, and variations of each.

MUSIC

Music is an integral part of the early childhood program. The expressive quality of music offers a powerful route to feelings. Music provides enjoyment in listening, singing, playing, and movement. The child should feel good about himself/herself; develop the ability to listen sensitively, move responsively, play simple instruments, and sing; develop a beginning understanding of musical elements; and appreciate music from other cultures. The teacher needs to provide daily music activities; a listening center; and opportunities for movement, performing, composing, and improvising.

CREATIVE MOVEMENT

The use of creative movement helps the child to develop body awareness, body isolation, body shape, and locomotor skills. Creative movement lets the child explore his/her own personal, creative, and innovative way of moving. The teacher should provide opportunities for children to explore the use of space and tempo through their individual expression. Creative movement should be used at every opportunity within the program.

The Whole Child

Combined, the four areas form the "whole child"—one who wants to discover, explore, and experiment with the world around him/her. Children build their knowledge on past experiences. Allowing children to discover who they are, and what part they play in the lives of others, will enhance this growth. Given these opportunities, a child will realize his/her worth physically, emotionally, socially, and intellectually. Children may seem very complex, but it must be remembered that they are actually very simple, and are each one of a kind. A child develops the inner self while gaining knowledge of his/her surroundings, and can then find a place within those surroundings. An early childhood teacher plays a major role in providing an environment that is conducive to discovery about who the child is. A teacher must be caring, loving, patient, and firm, but kind. An early childhood teacher must provide preschoolers with the opportunity and encouragement to develop at their own special rate and style. A special teacher who can provide children with the necessary foundation for all their future learning, whether intellectual or social, must be able to relate to students their own value as human beings.

Play

Although play, because of its importance, should be treated as a separate chapter, special consideration is given within the curriculum chapter because of its appropriate placement within the early childhood curriculum.

A child's play is his/her "work"—the basis for *all* learning. Only through play is a child free to make mistakes without risk, to try new ideas without fear of failure, to explore how something works without the necessity of making it work, to experiment without adult intervention, to be a part of an activity, to make the rules and change them, and to enjoy an activity totally. Children love to play, and find that the challenges within the activity are intriguing. The child seeks flexibility and may change the activity at any time without "risk" to himself/herself or the activity. Play provides mastery of one step at a time, and through it a child will pick the level of skill and challenge that he/she feels most comfortable exploring. A child plays to succeed, but if success is not attained there is still no failure perceived. The perception of the child is that everything was done just for fun, and thus the child becomes actively involved.

Play in the simplest to the most complex form supports: problem solving, a child's language and literacy, and expression of positive and negative emotions for the child. Play also contributes to the child's cognitive maturity by: providing opportunities to practice new skills while experiencing events; transforming reality into symbolic representations; consolidating previous learning; learning actively as a "whole child"; enabling him/her to learn about learning; developing creativity; and reducing the pressures and tension from correct and incorrect performance.

Teachers of young children have an important task in providing an appropriate curriculum that fosters play as an integral aspect of the daily curriculum content. Children do not all play equally. There are several factors that influence a child's play: the selectiveness of the child, differences of children's types of play, mood of the child, variation of style, differences in sex and social background, the interaction of the child with the parent and/or teacher, sibling and peer influences, material available, optimal environment, limitations of space, and placement of materials in the room. The placement of materials should always be on low open shelves within a child's reach (a toy box is the worst place to store toys).

After the teacher has considered the factors of influence, he/she must then structure the classroom to be conducive to play. To encourage play, the teacher can provide:

- toys that work properly and allow feedback to the child
- an environment that allows for free safe play
- enough toys and materials
- toys that are matched to the developmental level of the child
- emphasis on the process of play, not the product
- sensitive adults
- ample time to promote problem solving
- a minimum of interruptions
- the use of the materials by the children
- storage of materials that are accessible to children
- the willingness to allow children to be "messy"

When a teacher provides a room that promotes play, he/she has prepared a place where children feel free to explore.

At this point the teacher needs to evaluate his/her role within the curriculum. The teacher should be:

- an observer—helping the child only when the child needs help
- a supervisor—preparing a conducive room arrangement, offering feedback, and supporting the children
- a planner—providing a variety, amount, and range of materials for the child to use
- an evaluator—constantly assessing social, intellectual, emotional, and physical skills and growth

The teacher is an "observer," but not a player. Children need to be allowed the opportunity for their own exploration. Teachers can encourage involvement and act playful, but should not impose their ideas on the play activity. Allow time, space, and props, but do not interfere, whether play is real or imaginary.

As with all areas of the classroom, there will be problems that will need to be handled. Children who demonstrate unoccupied behavior may become bored. If so, provide help and new items to foster play. Children may exhibit merely observational behavior; if so, help integrate the child into a play situation. Children may demonstrate transition; if so, give the child time to change and provide advance clues of that change and make the new activity pleasurable. Children could exhibit aggression if the environment is too authoritarian or too small. If aggression does occur, make sure there are enough activities and that rules are fair, and provide ample time for children to resolve disagreements before the teacher interrupts.

Play is the cornerstone of the child's development and learning. The teacher is the vital link in providing an environment that encourages the child's ability to explore and play "risk-free" and naturally. There are many theories concerning play with which the teacher needs to be familiar. As with all development, play proceeds in stages. Teachers must be aware of these stages, so they can provide materials that foster appropriate development.

Remember, play is a child's work and it assists the child's appropriate development. A classroom where play is encouraged is an effective classroom and one that allows the child to build toward a fulfilled future. Everyone must play to sustain life, and providing a curriculum centered around play is appropriate for early childhood education.

Suggested Equipment List

CLASSROOM

Housekeeping Center

- children's stove, refrigerator, and sink (preferably wood)
- dishes, pots, pans, and utensils
- dolls, doll bed, and doll clothes
- dress-up clothes, such as: hats, shoes, purses, and jewelry
- rocker, child-size couch, and chairs
- play foods
- small tables and chairs
- telephones
- pillow
- mirror
- dust mop and broom

Library Center

- books
- book case (child-size)
- puppet theater
- carpeted floor
- bean bags
- rocking chair

Listening Center

- record player
- read along books
- cassette player
- carpet or bean bags
- headphones
- table and chairs
- all types of records and tapes

Blocks Center

- various sizes of large building blocks (wooden or cardboard; cardboard is safer for young children)
- figures of animals and humans
- toy trucks, cars, buses, trains, and planes
- Legos®, Tinkertoys®, Bristle Blocks®, and Lincoln Logs®
- small building blocks
- town set with people and cars
- airport, fire station, farm, etc.
- strawberry plastic baskets (available from grocery store)

Manipulative Center

- puzzles and pegboards
- letters and numbers
- flannelboard and sets

- beads for stringing
- teddy bear counters
- sewing cards
- small colored cubes (buttons)
- stacking toys
- parquet blocks or mosaic tile
- shape box
- lotto games
- pounding toys
- card games
- woodworking toys
- board and math games

Art Center

- vinyl flooring
- easel, and table and chairs
- Playdough®, slime, and clay
- crayon and markers
- pencils and chalk
- tempera paint and watercolors
- scissors
- paste or glue
- scraps of paper
- blank paper, all sizes
- blackboard
- paper punch
- strings and straws
- printing materials
- finger paints and various size brushes

Circle Time Center

- carpet squares
- bulletin board
- chalkboard
- adult rocking chair

- record player
- American flag
- calendar, helpers, and weather charts

Science Center

- aquarium
- live animals
- incubator
- rocks, shells, and minerals
- magnifying glass
- magnets
- balances
- measuring cups and spoons
- cooking utensils
- water or sand table
- sieves, pump, funnels, plastic bottles, cups, and plastic tubing

Active Indoor Play

- parachute or sheet
- foam balls
- balance beam
- exercise records
- piano
- jump ropes
- bean bags

PLAYGROUND

- swings, sling, tire (not plastic, because of danger) (make sure that swings are secure in the ground)
- sandbox (tractor tire) with sieves, cups, etc.
- commercial playground equipment (check for safety)
- tree stump with hammer, nails, screws, and screwdrivers
- wagons, tricycles, riding toys, and wheelbarrows
- large trucks, trains, cars, and tractors for playing in the sand
- jungle gym and monkey bars (check for safety)

- rubber balls (various sizes)
- rocker
- slide
- tire bouncers
- plastic bats and balls

Materials for Curriculum Areas

INTELLECTUAL

Math

- stacking blocks
- sorting balls
- pegboards
- parquet blocks
- beads
- spools for stringing
- colored cubes
- teddy bear counters
- plastic numbers
- mosaic tiles
- number set cards
- simple number games
- flannelboard with numbers and shapes
- calendar with month, day and the week, and date
- box buttons that can be sorted by size, shape, and color

Science

- magnifying glass
- balance
- water wheels
- cooking
- live animals
- pulleys
- incline blocks
- microscope

- aquarium
- hatch chickens
- grow plants
- field trips to farm, zoo, or orchard
- water experiments (ice to water)
- nature items (leaves, rocks, shells, bugs, etc.)
- flannelboard with animals and body parts

Social Studies

- bus ride
- role play
- dramatic play
- field trips to fire station, police station, post office, dentist, doctor, hospital, restaurants, bakery, and grocery store

Health

- try different foods
- make decisions
- visit doctor and hospital
- wash hands
- prepare snacks
- socialize with classmates
- be attentive in group time
- respect the rights of others
- sharing
- controlling emotions

COMMUNICATION

Language

- show and tell
- sharing time
- counting
- housekeeping
- block area

- manipulatives
- playing games
- finger plays
- stories
- puppet theater
- books to share
- snack time
- playground time
- working independently
- interaction with other children
- participating in group activities
- identifying capital and lowercase alphabet
- knowing address and phone number
- recognizing first name in print
- following directions

Pre-Reading Skills

- listening skills
- left-right orientation
- following oral directions
- attention span lengthens
- turning pages in book
- sequencing of story events
- labeling classroom
- library
- visual and auditory discrimination

Pre-Writing Skills

- labeling classroom
- coloring
- drawing
- painting
- oral to written story
- computer
- cutting
- using basic manuscript (try D'Lealian)
- writing first name only on unlined paper (lined paper should not be used until the end of kindergarten)

Literature

- library books
- reading stories to children
- role play books
- making children take books home
- chart stories
- create make believe stories
- visit the library
- story records
- writing children's own stories into book form
- listening center with books to read along

PHYSICAL

Sensory Development

- feely box
- parquet blocks
- nature walks
- listening
- touching
- smelling
- Playdough®
- water play
- sand
- mud
- clay
- shaving cream
- painting with pudding

Gross and Fine Motor

- puzzles
- pegboards
- Legos®
- Tinkertoys®
- Lincoln Logs®
- pouring and sifting
- painting

- bean bag games
- balance beam
- drawing and cutting
- pasting and gluing
- collages
- balls
- writing and typing
- parachute games
- relays
- soccer
- playing active games
- throwing and catching balls
- exercising to music
- fastening snaps, buttons, and zippers
- running, hopping, skipping, jumping, and climbing

CREATIVE

Art

- painting
- printing
- collages
- modeling
- drawing and coloring
- recognizing colors

Music

- singing
- playing and making instruments
- beating
- rhythm
- moving to music
- listening to all types of music

Drama

- role playing in housekeeping
- performing simple plays

Movement

- dancing
- exercising to music
- free form movement

Planning

The early childhood curriculum must be an ongoing process revolving around the child's individual development ability. The teacher is continually observing the child to determine skills the child has mastered, and skills that need improvement. The teacher defines the objectives and plans activities and experiences that will accomplish the objectives. Because each child may be at a different level of development, a teacher may be working on many areas of the process at one time. Lesson plans can be developed in units for class periods or weeks. However, experience dictates that general planning for the entire school year gives the teacher and parent a guide and foundation on which to build instruction.

Figure 47 outlines general unit areas and brief samples of activities that can be included. Specific dates and times are not included since these are only a guide and can be altered as necessary. The teacher has ample opportunity to expand on the units within the daily lesson plans. Figure 48 shows a sample monthly schedule of units.

WEEKLY LESSON PLANS

Some daily lessons are very detailed, while others include only general activities that are planned for the day. The school board should determine lesson plan requirements. However, practice and experience indicate that a teacher must have good plans for daily activities in order to provide the appropriate development activities for the children. Figure 49 shows such a daily lesson plan.

There are several excellent early childhood lesson plan books available. The preschool should purchase one for each teacher. The director should monitor the lesson plan books

Week	September	October	November	December	January
1	• Me, myself and I • Height and weight • Stick man • Trace body • Self portrait • Paper person	• Fall animals • Leaf people • Fall tree	• Food and food products • Edible playdough • Peanut butter	• Christmas • Angel • Reindeer • Santa • Stocking	• Winter fun • Bird feeder • Snow paint
2	• Home and family	• Leaf crayon rubbings	• Indians • Headbands • Teepees • Canoes	• Ginger bread men • Trees • Ornaments	• Finger paint on wax paper
3	• Color week • Shapes	• Halloween • Witches • Pumpkins • Ghosts	• Thanksgiving • Pilgrims	• Bell from dixie cups • Candy canes	• Sweat shirt week
4	• Health • Manners • Grooming	• Masks • Party	• Foods • Cornucopia • Freedom • Ice water experiment	• Party	• Winter feely box feast

Figure 47. Example of general lesson plans (September–January).

(continued)

Week	February	March	April	May	Notes
1	• Valentines • Hearts • Valentines • Flags	• Foreign neighbors • Chinese hats • Animals from other countries	• Easter • Spring • Hatch chickens	• Mother's Day • Circus theme animals • Lion with yarn mane	
2	• Cards • Party	• Community helpers • Hospital trip	• Plant gardens • New life	• Clowns • Paint clown faces	
3	• Musical instruments	• Fireman • Police • St. Patrick's Day	• Farm animals • Spring walks	• Graduation party	
4	• Human body	• Safety	• Hat week		

Figure 47 (continued). Example of general lesson plans (February–March).

regularly to ascertain their correct use. Good plans build quality programs, therefore teachers must plan accordingly and write these plans down, adding or deleting ideas as needed.

Teachers should have freedom within their classroom and activities, but the director must be very aware of what is being taught and planned within the school. The director's duties are not to control, but to guide each teacher in planning the appropriate activities that provide the children with the skills and experiences that foster physical, intellectual, social, and creative development.

Skills

The director and teachers should determine the skills to be experienced and mastered by children during the school year.

AUGUST: Clowns, folder work

SEPTEMBER: T-Shirt day, color week, apples, leaf (colored tissue) squirrels, nuts, field trip to orchard

OCTOBER: Witches, ghosts, masks, pumpkins, stuffed animal day, Halloween party, field trip

NOVEMBER: Turkey, Indians, horn of plenty, hats, pilgrims, feast, conferences, field trip

DECEMBER: Angels, candy canes, stockings, Santa, presents for parents, field trip, Christmas program and party

JANUARY: Snow, Frosty, New Year's Day, sweatshirt day

FEBRUARY: Valentine's Day, conferences, Presidents' Day, Valentine's Day party, field trip to post office

MARCH: St. Patrick's Day, wind, nature day, kites, start ABC books, field trip to museum

APRIL: Showers, plant flowers for Mother's Day, hatch chickens, Easter party, field trip, hat day, folder work

MAY: Mother's Day cards, second color week, picnic, field day

---

Figure 48. Example of monthly schedule of units.

Skill development should follow the curriculum areas. The skills should be listed as they are introduced and reinforced through regular activities. The lists should serve only as a general guide to provide direction.

Parents need to be given copies of the skill lists at the beginning of the school year, enabling the teacher and parents to share communication concerning the skills to be taught. These skills are often termed "readiness skills," implying they must be reinforced throughout the year, which will prepare

ABC Preschool WEEK OF _____			
	8:00–8:35	8:35–9:00	9:00–9:45
Monday	• Greeting (calendar, Pledge, weather, and read book)	• Color sheet • Practice cutting	• Learning centers • Learn rules
Tuesday	• Greeting	• Practice cutting on the lines	• Learning centers
Wednesday	• Greeting	• Color rocket • Check for color knowledge	• Learning centers
Thursday	• Greeting	• Talk about your house, address • Draw house and write address, phone number at bottom	• Learning centers
Friday	• Greeting • Talk about cooperation	• Make paper plate bears	• Learning centers

Figure 49. *Example of daily lesson plans.*

Skills introduced and reinforced through regularly scheduled art, music, library, and various "fun" activities.

RESPONSIBILITY FOR: self, classmates, room
SEPARATION FROM: mother, father, sibling, etc.
SOCIAL DEVELOPMENT: sharing, caring, making friends, etc.
PHYSICAL COORDINATION:

(1) Rhythms, rhymes, finger-plays, songs, exercises

(2) Painting, coloring, pasting, cutting, stringing beads, and various other manipulative activities

PERSONALITY AND CHARACTER DEVELOPMENT: morals, being your own person, respecting the rights of others and rights of self

LEARNING SELF-CONTROL: lengthening attention span, following directions, expanding listening skills, asserting control over one's own emotions and actions

ABC Preschool

Dear Parents,

This first school experience for your child is an important one. Thus, it is our purpose to make this experience enjoyable, educational, developmental, and on-going. The preceding list outlines our three year program, which is geared to provide a total readiness experience to better prepare your child for his/her future in the continuing educational programs.

If at any time you have questions or suggestions, please feel free to call.

Sincerely,

Three Year Teachers

Figure 50. Example of class skills—three year class.

ABC Preschool

Dear Parents,

Welcome to ABC Preschool. During the year we will be working on numerous skills that will prepare your child for entering Kindergarten. Below is a list of these skills.

Counting	Manners
Number recognition	Days of week, seasons
Number concepts	Months, holidays
Left and right hands	Small motor skills (cutting, coloring, etc.)
Print first name	
Print alphabet	Children's games and songs
Recognize colors	Rhyming words
Recognize alphabet	Attempt new tasks
Patience	Enter group play
Sharing	Adjust to group play
Opposites	Sequencing
Home address	Home phone number
Increased attention span	Expanded vocabulary
Enter class conversations	

Each of these skills will be introduced in a fun way. We want your child to enjoy his/her first school experience and do not want undue pressure placed upon him/her. The above skills will be introduced, and when your child is ready he/she will be able to do each one.

If your child's work is not what *you* expect, please remember that every child must develop at his/her own rate and pace here at ABC. We do not judge children as a group, but as individuals.

Please help us by praising your child's work and play, and if you ever have any questions or concerns, please call us so we can discuss them.

Together let's make this first school experience one that your child will cherish.

Sincerely,

Four Year Teachers

Figure 51. Skill sheet for younger four-year-olds.

the child for the next stage of development. Figures 50–53 show examples of such skills lists.

Evaluation

Even for early childhood programs a teacher must evaluate the child's progress. Evaluation instruments range from very specific, formal documents to teacher-made informal in-

---

Dear Parents,

Here is a brief list of some things your child will learn through the fun time activities this year:

Counting 1–30
Recognizing numbers
Concept of numbers
Knowing left from right
Printing first name
Colors
Some geometric figures
Coins
Home address, birthdate, age, phone number, days of the week, seasons, and months of the year
Handwork (cut, paste, color, and paint)
Children's games and dances
Increasing attention span
Expanding vocabulary
Taking part in class conversations
Alphabet (phonics)
Trying new tasks
Adjusting and entering into group play

We understand that your child's future in the educational system depends upon his/her preschool preparedness. If you have any questions or suggestions, please feel free to call us.

Sincerely,

Four Year Teachers

Figure 52. Four year class skill sheet.

ABC Preschool

Dear Parents,

We understand that your child's future depends upon his/her preschool readiness experiences. The importance of the school is the role it plays in developing each individual child.

We hope to fulfill this role by carrying out activities in the following skill areas:

ALPHABET: Recognition and phonetic skills
NUMBERS: 1–30/Recognition, concept, and counting skills
COLORS: Colors and color words
GEOMETRIC PICTURES
VOCABULARY: Increase vocabulary and expand verbal skills
MUSIC: Games, dances, songs, and finger-plays
ART: Cutting, pasting, coloring, painting, and creative activities
WRITING: Printing first name, letters, and numbers 1–10
PHYSICAL EXERCISE
CALENDAR: Months, days, and seasons
SELF-HELP SKILLS: Home address, phone number, birthdate, age, use of scissors, tie shoes, expression of feelings, development of self-concept

We are looking forward to working with your child during this important time in his/her life. If you have any questions, please feel free to call.

Sincerely,

Pre-Kindergarten Teachers

Figure 53. Pre-Kindergarten skill list.

struments. All types should be examined and from this examination the director and teachers can determine the specific needs of each program. An instrument can be developed that provides specific information regarding skills the program stresses. Before selecting an instrument or system of evaluation, the school board and director should examine the school policy and purpose, and determine which skills the program expects the children to experience and ultimately master.

When preparing and sharing with parents the particular

evaluation instruments, remember that every child develops at his/her own rate. Do not become so technical that the evaluation instrument is not understood by parents and teachers, and be certain that it measures correctly the items it was designed to measure. Included in Figures 54–56 are sample evaluations for various classes. These should be used as a guide permitting each program to carefully determine their individual needs.

ABC Preschool

Code: Y = Yes   N = No

_____   Follows teacher's directions
_____   Obeys quickly and cheerfully
_____   Listens attentively to stories and poems
_____   Can work alone
_____   Feels good about self
_____   Takes care of wraps
_____   Takes care of school material
_____   Shows love for others
_____   Works and plays well with others
_____   Can share ideas
_____   Waits turn
_____   Enjoys and participates in songs and finger-plays
_____   Enjoys and participates in rhythms and games
_____   Enjoys art activities
_____   Uses hands well: cutting, drawing, pasting, etc.
_____   Knows basic colors: red, blue, green, yellow, orange, purple, black, brown, white
_____   Recognizes number 1–10
_____   Counts 1–10
_____   Recognizes alphabet: A B C D E F G H I J K L M N O P Q R S T U V W X Y Z
_____   Recites alphabet
_____   Recognizes sizes: large, medium, small, tall, short
_____   Recognizes basic shapes: square, circle, rectangle, triangle
_____   Recognizes printed name (first name only)
_____   Knows address
_____   Knows whole name
_____   Knows Mother's and Father's first names

Figure 54. Example of three-year-old progress report.

```
ABC Preschool

Code:  + Achieved      −   Need Improvement
       = Progressing   NA  Not Introduced at This Time

Student's Name: _____
Birthday: _____


FALL    SPRING
                     THE CHILD
_____  _____   1. Recognizes his/her printed name
_____  _____   2. States his/her full name
_____  _____   3. Prints his/her first name
_____  _____   4. States his/her address
_____  _____   5. States his/her phone number
                     SOCIAL SKILLS
_____  _____   6. Follows directions
_____  _____   7. Is attentive at group time
_____  _____   8. Works by self with no help required
_____  _____   9. Requires encouragement to complete
                     task
_____  _____  10. Gets along well with classmates
                     MOTOR CONTROL
_____  _____  11. Grasps pencil or crayon correctly
_____  _____  12. Colors within lines
_____  _____  13. Holds scissors correctly
_____  _____  14. Cuts with control
_____  _____  15. Catches ball with both hands
_____  _____  16. Bounces ball
_____  _____  17. Walks forward on balance beam
                     without help
_____  _____  18. Gallops
```

Figure 55. Example of four-year-old progress report.

_____	_____	19. Skips
_____	_____	20. Hops
		IDENTIFIES COLORS
_____	_____	21. Red
_____	_____	22. Yellow
_____	_____	23. Blue
_____	_____	24. Green
_____	_____	25. Purple
_____	_____	26. Orange
_____	_____	27. Black
_____	_____	28. Brown
_____	_____	29. White
_____	_____	30. Pink
		IDENTIFIES BASIC SHAPES
_____	_____	31. Circle
_____	_____	32. Square
_____	_____	33. Rectangle
_____	_____	34. Triangle
_____	_____	35. Identifies capital letters of the alphabet
_____	_____	None of the letters
_____	_____	Some of the letters
_____	_____	Most of the letters
_____	_____	All of the letters
		NUMBER KNOWLEDGE
_____	_____	36. Counts, one by one to
_____	_____	37. Can print numbers 0–5
_____	_____	38. Can print numbers 6–10
		HEIGHT AND WEIGHT
		May _____
		September _____
		Growth _____

Figure 55 (continued). Example of four-year-old progress report.

ABC Preschool

Code:
 A Always   N Never
 U Usually   NA Not applicable
 S Sometimes

Student's Name: _____

Birthday: _____

Fall Winter Spring

THE CHILD

_____ 1. Recognizes his/her first name

_____ 2. States his/her last name

_____ 3. Prints his/her first name

_____ 4. Prints his/her last name

_____ 5. States his/her address

_____ 6. States his/her phone number

SOCIAL SKILLS

_____ 7. Follows directions involving one or two steps

_____ 8. Is attentive at group time

_____ 9. Works by self with no help required

_____ 10. Gets along well with classmates

_____ 11. Accepts classroom responsibility

_____ 12. Participates in group activities

IDENTIFIES THE FOLLOWING

_____ 13. Red

_____ 14. Yellow

_____ 15. Blue

_____ 16. Green

_____ 17. Purple

_____ 18. Orange

_____ 19. Black

_____ 20. Brown

_____ 21. White

_____ 22. Pink

_____ 23. Grey

IDENTIFIES

_____ 24. Circle

_____ 25. Square

_____ 26. Rectangle

_____ 27. Triangle

Figure 56. Example of readiness progress report.

REPRODUCES

_____ 28. Circle

_____ 29. Square

_____ 30. Rectangle

_____ 31. Triangle

MOTOR SKILLS

_____ 32. Kicks ball without losing balance

_____ 33. Throws ball accurately

_____ 34. Catches ball

_____ 35. Skips

_____ 36. Gallops

_____ 37. Bounces ball with control

_____ 38. Walks forward on balance beam using
hands to balance

_____ 39. Grasps pencil or crayon correctly

_____ 40. Colors within lines

_____ 41. Completes simple insert puzzle

_____ 42. Holds scissors correctly

_____ 43. Cuts on dotted lines

NUMBER KNOWLEDGE

_____ 44. Counts one by one, to

_____ 45. Can produce numbers 0–5 on request

_____ 46. Can reproduce 6–10 on request

_____ 47. Gives verbal name for numerals

_____ 48. Demonstrates one-to-one
correspondence

_____ 49. Describes given sets as more than,
less than

_____ 50. States days of the week in sequence

_____ 51. States months of the year in
sequence

THE ALPHABET

_____ 52. Identifies capital letters of the
alphabet

_____ 53. Identifies lowercase letters of the
alphabet

_____ 54. Matches capital and lowercase letters
of the alphabet

Figure 56 (continued). Examples of readiness progress report.

School

It is important that parents have an opportunity to evaluate the preschool program. Many excellent ideas have been gained from parent evaluations, and they have also given parents a chance to air their particular gripes. The evaluation form should be simple and not time consuming. Signatures should not be required, because parents should feel free to express their true feelings.

The parent evaluation form can be used to improve the quality of a program. Parents' input is of great importance, because parents know what they want for their children from the school. Only about 20% of these forms will be returned, but the value of those returned is immeasurable as a key to program improvement.

Major program changes should only be made after a number of negative comments have been received on particular items. If there is only one negative comment for a given area, look closely at the reasons—but this usually is not enough justification to make a radical change. If there are two to three, examine the problem very closely and make a decision based on these findings. If there are four or more, immediately realize that there is a problem, and examine this area closely with changes in mind. Occasionally, even a program that has many negative comments should be continued if the positive comments outweigh the negative ones. Many times new programs receive negative responses, but if given sufficient time to grow, will later find value within the program.

Figure 57 is an example of a parent evaluation form. Use class codes on the forms to ascertain which programs are being discussed by the parents.

Miscellaneous

Each year, notify the elementary schools concerning any potential children from the program who will be attending their program the coming year. This should be done as a courtesy to the schools. An example of this type of letter is shown in Figures 58 and 59.

ABC Preschool

MID-YEAR EVALUATION FORM

Please fill out and return to school as soon as possible. I will read and evaluate each one of these.

I ask for a truthful evaluation of our programs. Help our staff to continue to improve and offer you the best in education for your child. Please give me all of your comments (good or bad). Signatures are not required.

Thank you,

Director

---

1. Loading and unloading:

2. Child's educational program:

3. Communication between you and teacher:

4. Your personal comments:

5. Director:

Figure 57. Example of parent evaluation form.

ABC Preschool

Dear _____ School:

Enclosed is a list of children who attended ABC preschool and have enrolled in your Kindergarten Program for the 19___ school year. All are anxiously awaiting the fall and their "big" school experience.

The experiences they have had with us were varied. ABC Preschool, licensed by the State Department of Education, provided each child with a complete readiness program that prepared him/her for the kindergarten year to come. The program included all areas of a readiness curriculum without infringing upon the kindergarten program.

It was the goal of our school to prepare each child so that the school experience would be anticipated with an open, creative mind, receptive to the new exciting world of learning to which they will be exposed during their kindergarten year. It is our hope that the training they have received from ABC Preschool will make their transition to kindergarten smoother for both them and you.

If at any time I can be of assistance concerning a child's past school experiences or performances, please feel free to contact me.

Sincerely,

Director

Figure 58. Example of a letter to elementary schools.

ABC Preschool

Dear Principal:

Our records indicate that the following child is enrolled in your school for the coming year. Enclosed you will find a progress report and our school record information. Parents of the child are to bring with them a copy of the birth certificate and immunization record when they enroll their child in your school.

If you have any questions, feel free to call me.

Sincerely,

Director

ABC Kindergarten Information Form

Child's Name: _____

Birthdate: _____

Address: _____

_____

Phone: _____

Parents: _____

Teacher's Comments: _____

_____

_____

Date: _____

Figure 59. *Example of school report.*

Suggested Books

This chapter briefly described an early childhood curriculum and is only a starting point for a good program. To gain a more in-depth knowledge, the following books are suggested.

(1) Books about the Stages of Development by Jean Piaget
(2) *The Early Childhood Teachers Almanack* by Newmann
(3) *Group Games in Early Education* by Kamii and De Vries
(4) *I Can Do It, I Can Do It* by Gilbert
(5) *Progressive Education Inquiry Method* by John Dewey
(6) *Who Am I? In the Lives of Children* by Feeney, Christensen, and Moravcik
(7) *Years to Grow* by Yemm and Dennison
(8) *The Young Child—Reviews of Research* by Willard
(9) *Young Children with Special Needs* by Thurman and Weiderstrom

The National Association for the Education of Young Children (NAEYC) is an excellent source. Some of the books they offer are:

(1) *The Cognitive Oriented Curriculum*, NAEYC
(2) *Language in Early Childhood Education* by Carden, NAEYC
(3) *Numbers in Preschool and Kindergarten*, NAEYC
(4) *Science with Young Children*, NAEYC

For many of the ideas in this chapter, the authors are indebted to the following source:

Feeney, S., D. Christensen and E. Moravcik. 1983. *Who Am I? In the Lives of Children: An Introduction to Teaching Young Children (2nd edition)*. Columbus, OH: Merrill.

Readers seeking further information or clarification should consult this excellent work.

CHAPTER EIGHT

Staffing

> IF YOU TREAT MEN THE WAY THEY ARE
> YOU NEVER IMPROVE THEM.
> IF YOU TREAT THEM THE WAY YOU WANT THEM TO BE, YOU DO.
> —Goethe

THIS chapter is intended as a guide to the director and school board in the recruitment and retention of staff. The staff members of each school, whether teachers, assistants, or others, will be the people with whom parents regularly deal. Staff should be chosen very carefully, not only for their educational background, but for their professional mannerisms, their personality, and their sense of caring for children. Teachers and assistants should not be required to possess a college degree in education, but they must care for children and demonstrate that caring daily.

Teachers who do not have college degrees should first serve as classroom assistants, and demonstrate their teaching abilities while serving as teaching assistants. When teacher openings occur, the assistants should be given the opportunity to move up to teaching positions and to demonstrate their teaching abilities. Within a year, through in-service training and guidance from the director, teaching assistants can develop programs that are educationally and developmentally sound. In most preschools, teachers and assistants team-teach, so it is not unusual for an assistant to have all the knowledge and experience necessary to move up to full teacher. This promotion from within will keep a program educationally, developmentally, and structurally sound. It will also keep the program attuned to the policies of the school. These advantages must continually be balanced against the most obvious disadvantage, program "inbreeding." Regardless of program quality, every preschool occasionally needs an influx of "new blood" to overcome the stagnation and complacency that often results from familiarity. Therefore, the director and school board must bal-

127

ance loyalty to teaching assistants against the opportunity for revitalization, creativity, and change.

A degreed teacher is not always the best choice, but is really the first choice. If someone has demonstrated abilities as a teaching assistant, give that person a chance to grow. When promotion is done from within the preschool, the director should be in continual contact with the new teacher and ascertain that his/her instructional methods are educationally sound.

The Teacher

The following guidelines have been developed over many years of experience. As previously stated, they are not hard-set rules. Each school should set its own guidelines, and decide, when the occasion arises, what deviation will be tolerated. The guidelines should be developed by the director and approved by the board of directors. All guidelines should begin with a job description. The job description should state:

(1) The purpose and policies of the school
(2) The expectations of the position
(3) The qualifications desired
(4) The responsibilities of the teacher
   • class management
   • professional conduct
   • absenteeism
   • professional growth
(5) The procedure for resolving dissention

An example of such a description is shown in Figure 60.

Assistants

Assistants are assigned to work closely with the teacher. If possible the teacher should be allowed to assist in the selection of his/her assistant. Harmony is needed within the classroom, and team-teaching should be used whenever possible.

ABC Preschool

TEACHER JOB DESCRIPTION

PURPOSE OF THE SCHOOL:

ABC Preschool is a nonprofit organization operating for the purpose of providing families in the community with a safe, loving atmosphere for their children. Programs also provide the child with socialization, creative play, art, music, story time, physical activities, and educational learning experiences geared to the individual child's age and ability.

The school admits students of any race, color, national and ethnic origins to all the rights, privileges, programs, and activities generally accorded or made available to the students of the school.

JOB DESCRIPTION: Teacher—Preschool:

The person selected for this position will be responsible for the general supervision and management of a class of children between three and five years of age.

QUALIFICATIONS:

The person selected for this position will be professionally prepared as a teacher of young children, especially in the field of early childhood education/development, or will have sufficient experience, as determined by the school board.

RESPONSIBILITIES:

Responsibilities will include, but will not be limited to, the following:

A. Class Management:
    1. Planning, supervising, and implementing the program for the class in accordance with the policies and philosophy of ABC Preschool, as specified in the handbook.
    2. Reporting and clearing activities, programs, trips, and educational procedures through the director.
    3. Clearing *all* requests for expenditures through the director.
    4. Gearing the program to the needs of the individual child with concerns for his/her interests, special talents, and individual style and pace of learning.

(continued)

Figure 60. Example of teacher job description.

5. Assisting in public relations events sponsored by the school.
6. Being responsible for the ordered arrangement, appearance, decor, and learning environment of the classroom.
7. Assuming an equal share of the joint housekeeping responsibilities of the staff.
8. Being responsible for the orderly loading/unloading of the children.

B. Professional Conduct:
1. Working in professional harmony with children, parents, and all other staff members.
2. Treating each child with dignity and respect.
3. Implementing methods for effectively utilizing the services of classroom assistants whether paid or volunteer.
4. Planning and implementing methods of establishing a positive liaison with parents of students.
5. Being in the classroom fifteen minutes prior to the opening of school and remaining until all the children in your class are gone, unless you are released by the director.

C. Absenteeism:
1. Call director if you are unable to attend school.
2. You will be allowed one working week worth of paid sick days per year. (A working week consists of the total number of hours in class time per week.)
3. Excessive absenteeism (as determined by the school board) will be grounds for termination of contract.
4. Sick leave is noncumulative.

D. Professional Growth:
1. Attending all staff meetings.
2. Participating in recommended training programs, conferences, courses, and other aspects of professional growth.

E. Dissention:
1. If concerns, problems, or dissentions occur within the staff, it is the duty of each staff member to discuss said concerns with the director and/or the school board immediately. It is then the duty of each person involved to consider viable solutions to the concerns and diligently work in a professional manner to solve the problems as quickly as possible for the good of all concerned.

Figure 60 (continued). Example of teacher job description.

An assistant's job should not consist merely of the dirty or "run fetch" work; it should be a team effort.

The teaching assistant's job description should state:

(1) The purpose and policies of the school
(2) The expectation of the position
(3) The qualifications desired for the position
(4) The responsibilities of the teaching assistant
   • class management
   • professional conduct
   • absenteeism
   • professional growth
(5) A statement as to the procedure for resolving dissention

Figure 61 outlines this sort of job description.

Recruitment

Staff members can be recruited in many ways—newspaper advertisements, fellow employees, organizations, and parent information. All of these methods can and should be utilized. Staff members can be recruited by knowing a member of the current staff, a parent of an enrolled child, members of professional organizations, and from advertising. There is no one best way, but staff longevity has been better when employees were recruited from the parents of former students and from staff recommendations. Even hiring from newspaper advertisements can produce employees who are well qualified and who work well within the program.

The director should always keep his/her ears open for people who would work well in the preschool program, because a position may open at any time in the future. Good people are not hard to find if you have been looking for them.

An application should be developed for use when people inquire about a job. Resumes can also be used, but experience has shown that applications are better because specific questions are addressed that are important to each individual program. Applications should be prepared carefully, and the questions on the application must be nondiscriminatory. Some

ABC Preschool

TEACHING ASSISTANT JOB DESCRIPTION

PURPOSE OF THE SCHOOL:

ABC Preschool is a nonprofit organization operating for the purpose of providing families in the community with a safe, loving atmosphere for their children. Programs also provide the child with socialization, creative play, art, music, story time, physical activities, and educational learning experiences geared to the individual child's age and ability.

The school admits students of any race, color, national and ethnic origins to all the rights, privileges, programs, and activities generally accorded or made available to the students of the school.

JOB DESCRIPTION: Assistant—Preschool:

The person selected for this position will be responsible for assisting the classroom teacher in the general supervision and management of a class of children between three and five years of age.

QUALIFICATIONS:

The person selected for this position must have a warm and friendly personality, be sensitive to feelings and needs of others, be able to relate well to children, and be willing to fulfill the responsibilities in accordance with the school's educational philosophy.

RESPONSIBILITIES:

Responsibilities will include, but will not be limited to, the following:

A. Class Management:
   1. Assisting in planning and implementing all aspects of the daily program under the direction of the teacher.

Figure 61. Example of teaching assistant job description.

2. Assisting in planning and preparing the learning environment, setting up interest centers, and preparing needed materials and supplies.
3. Supervising the classroom when the teacher is out of the room.
4. Helping with the general housekeeping tasks of the classroom.

B. Professional Conduct:
1. Working in professional harmony with children, parents, and all other staff members.
2. Treating each child with dignity and respect.
3. Maintaining professional attitudes.
4. Being in the classroom fifteen minutes prior to the opening of school and remaining until released by the teacher.

C. Absenteeism:
1. Call the director and teacher if unable to attend school.
2. You will be allowed one working week of paid sick days per year. (A working week consists of the total number of hours in class time per week.)
3. Excessive absenteeism (as determined by the school board) will be grounds for termination of contract.
4. Sick leave is noncumulative.

D. Professional Growth:
1. Attending all staff meetings.
2. Participating in recommended training programs, conferences, courses, and other aspects of professional growth.

E. Dissention:
1. If concerns, problems, or dissentions occur within the staff, it is the duty of each staff member to discuss the concerns with the director and/or the school board immediately. It is then the duty of each person involved to consider viable solutions and diligently work in a professional manner to solve the problems as quickly as possible for the good of all concerned.

Figure 61 (continued). Example of teaching assistant job description.

```
┌─────────────────────────────────────────────────────────────┐
│                      ABC Preschool                          │
│                                                             │
│              APPLICATION FOR EMPLOYMENT                     │
│                                                             │
│  Position applying for: _____  │
│  Name: _____  │
│  Address: _____  │
│  Last T.B. Test: _____  Last Physical Exam: _____  │
│                     (date)                         (date)  │
│                                                             │
│  EDUCATION:                                                 │
│  High School                                                │
│  Name: _____  │
│  Address: _____  │
│  Dates Attended: _____  │
│                                                             │
│  College/Trade Schools                                      │
│  Name            Address              Dates  Attended      │
│  _____ │
│  _____ │
│  _____ │
│                                                             │
│  State License, Certificates, or Credentials:              │
│  _____ │
│  _____ │
│  _____ │
│                                                             │
│  Awards and/or Published Materials:                        │
│  _____ │
│  _____ │
│                                                             │
│  Courses taken that you feel qualify you for this position, │
│  list course title and subject and school:                 │
│  _____ │
│  _____ │
│                                                             │
│  List of Special Skills or Talents you possess:            │
│  _____ │
│  _____ │
│  _____ │
│                                                             │
│  Professional Organization Affiliation: (list)             │
│  _____ │
│  _____ │
│  _____ │
└─────────────────────────────────────────────────────────────┘
```

Figure 62. Example of employment application.

WORK EXPERIENCE: (Volunteer or Paid)

Employer Name/ Address	Job Description	From— To	Salary	Reason for Leaving

REFERENCES:
Name and Address, Title, Phone
Professional (list two)

_____

_____

Personal (list 2)

_____

_____

Have you ever been convicted of child abuse? ____ yes ____ no

Have you ever been convicted of a crime? _____ yes _____ no

If so when? _____ Where? _____

Why? _____

Outcome? _____

Why do you desire this position?

_____

_____

_____

What do you feel most qualifies you for this position?

_____

_____

_____

Would you be willing to attend in-services, special courses, workshops, or training programs that may be recommended?

_____

_____

Figure 62 (continued). *Example of employment application.*

preschool programs are now using genuine application forms that can be obtained at any office supply store. Others use the application form from the local public school district. Completed applications should be kept on file for future use. A sample form is shown in Figure 62.

Federal Laws Governing Personnel

When setting up the program, and prior to hiring a staff, both federal and state labor laws should be consulted. For information concerning each, contact:

- Federal–Department of Labor, Washington, D.C.
- State–Department of Labor within each state.

Minimum Wage

The minimum wage is set by the Federal Government on an hourly rate. The Department of Labor keeps employers updated on the minimum wage rate and any changes as they occur. If an employee works more than a forty-hour week, the employee must be paid time and a half. Even though a preschool staff usually will not work over forty hours per week, this regulation is an important one to remember.

Workman's Compensation Insurance

Every state requires that an employer carry this insurance to cover employees if they are injured while at work. The premiums for this insurance are rising dramatically each year. Check with an insurance agent concerning cost prior to developing a budget.

Unemployment Insurance

By law, all employers who are not tax-exempt must provide this benefit for all employees. This insurance is designed to provide an income to employees who lose their jobs because of economic reasons. This compensation is typically not provided to employees who are dismissed because of misconduct. A preschool with a tax-exempt status is not required to provide unemployment insurance.

Affirmative Action

Any business that has fifteen or more employees is subject to the Civil Rights Act of 1964. This law mandates, among other things, the right of an applicant to have equal opportunity in employment. The law provides certain restrictions on advertisement of job openings and how interviews are conducted, including the range of questions that can be asked. This law is amended from time to time, so check with the local Labor Relations Board if an employment procedure is in question.

Each preschool program is required to file a Nondiscriminatory Statement Form yearly. When this form is received, answer all the questions completely and return it to the address provided. Failure to comply will affect the tax-exempt status of the program, if such exists. Although the Civil Rights Act of 1964 applies only to preschools or businesses with fifteen or more employees, a school board and director would be advised to follow the guidelines of the affirmative action regulations.

Advertising

All job openings must be posted or advertised in a newspaper which includes an E.O.E. (Equal Opportunity Employer) statement in the advertisement. Advertising in this manner does not eliminate personal recommendations or resumes received prior to an opening. Wording in an advertisement should not contain job requirements relating to: gender, race, religion (there is an exception to this—religious organizations may specify that applicants of a specific religious orientation will be given priority consideration), or other qualifications that may be discriminatory. Public Law 94-142 also requires nondiscrimination against handicapped persons who qualify for employment.

Qualifications for the position must be stated so they are not perceived to favor (or discriminate against) one particular race, color, religion, gender, nationality, or age group. Advertisements cannot require photos (after an applicant is hired a photograph may be requested), birth certificates, naturalization papers, or any other document that may indicate race, sex, nationality, religion, or age.

Interview

PREPARING FOR THE INTERVIEW

A good starting point in the interviewing process is to appoint a panel to help do the interviewing. A good combination would be a staff member, a board member, and the director.

(1) Make sure to keep careful records of the interview in case of a discrimination accusation.
(2) The same questions should be asked of all the applicants. Every member of the interviewing committee should have a copy of the questions to be asked.
(3) The applicant may be asked to clarify any information written on the application.

The following are examples of questions that should be avoided in an interview:

(1) Have you changed your legal name?
(2) What was your maiden name?
(3) Who do you live with?
(4) Do you own or rent your home?

Make sure the person interviewed has a resume or application on file before the interview. This gives the applicant a chance to articulate his/her qualifications, and permits applicants to be screened and their references to be checked. References should be checked by letter or telephone. A sample verification letter can be seen in Figure 63, and a reference evaluation in Figure 64.

THE INTERVIEW

An interview often lasts for one hour or more. The interview schedule should allow enough time to talk freely with each applicant.

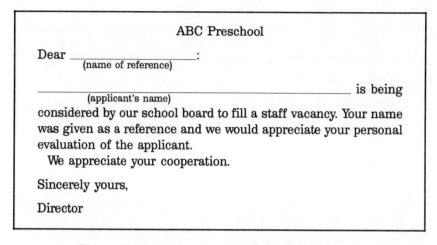

> ABC Preschool
>
> Dear _____:
>   (name of reference)
>
> _____ is being
>   (applicant's name)
> considered by our school board to fill a staff vacancy. Your name
> was given as a reference and we would appreciate your personal
> evaluation of the applicant.
>   We appreciate your cooperation.
>
> Sincerely yours,
>
> Director

Figure 63. Example of a reference verification letter.

The director should go over the job description, expectations, and responsibilities with each applicant. The director and/or interview committee should discuss the following: policies and procedures of the school, salary benefits, and work schedule. Also, the applicant should be given a class schedule and some expected activities of a typical day within the classroom.

Giving applicants a classroom situation, and asking how they would handle it, is a good way of finding out if their views will blend into your program. The educational program and requirements that each class is asked to fulfill should be explained. Time should also be allowed for the applicant to ask questions. The interview should be informal, but it is important to gain as much information as possible from the applicant.

Those who applied for positions and are *not hired* should be notified by letter regarding their status, and told that their application and/or resume will be retained for possible staff openings in the future.

Contract

In developing an employment contract, the following items should be considered:

ABC Preschool

Please give us your opinion of the applicant's ability in each of the following areas:

Relations with:

Administration: _____

_____

Staff: _____

_____

Parents: _____

_____

Children: _____

_____

Equipment: _____

_____

Instructional techniques: _____

_____

Professional conduct: _____

_____

Professional growth: _____

_____

How do you know the applicant? _____

_____

When did you know the applicant? _____

_____

If you were a former employer please complete the following:
  Applicant's position: _____
  Reason for leaving: _____

Additional comments: _____

_____

Signature: _____
Title: _____
Date: _____

Figure 64. *Example of a reference evaluation.*

(1) Give the name and location of the school issuing the contract.

(2) State the full name of the employee.

(3) State the period of the contract (issuance for the nine-month school year works well). Thus every staff member must renew his/her contract at the beginning of each school year.

(4) Define the specific position being offered.

(5) State the wage or rate that can be given monthly, daily, or hourly.

(6) List the terms of the contract.

(7) Give the signing date of employee and the school board.

(8) Include the signatures of employee, director, and others deemed necessary to sign (such as the chairperson of the school board).

Remember, a written contract is not worth the paper it is written on. The only binding contract is the recording in the official minutes of the school board. See Figure 65 for a sample contract.

Medical Reports

Most states require that all new staff members have a tuberculosis test, which must be kept with their contracts, in the director's personnel files. Tuberculosis tests need to be retaken every two to five years. The school board should set up a procedure concerning medical physicals and tuberculosis tests. State regulations need to be carefully checked to be sure that these guidelines are being met in the program.

Child Abuse Statement

In many states it is now required that people working with young children sign a child abuse disclaimer statement. This statement must read as such and must be kept in the employee's file. Figure 66 shows an example of such a form.

ABC Preschool

EMPLOYMENT CONTRACT

ABC Preschool of _____

and _____ as employee,

enter into this employment contract upon the following terms and conditions:

Period of Contract: _____

Position: _____

Rate of Wage: _____

By signing this contract, the employee is obligated to perform faithfully the services in accordance with the rules and regulations of the school, and specified in the school handbook, which is to be considered a part of the contract. The employee expresses the determination to work toward greater competence in teaching and to maintain a professional classroom.

By signing this contract, the school board and the director pledge to give cooperation, support, and respect.

Signed in duplicate this _____ day of _____ 19___.

_____   _____
Employee   Director

_____
Chairperson of School Board

Figure 65. Example of an employment contract.

I _____ have never been convicted of
    (employee's name)
child abuse or child molestation.

Signed: _____

Dated: _____

Each new employee should present an FBI fingerprint record to the director prior to being offered a contract.

Expense at employee cost for fingerprint examination.

Figure 66. Example of child abuse statement.

Some states are now requiring a Federal Bureau of Investigation (FBI) fingerprint analysis before employment. Be sure to check local and state regulations.

Assignment of Staff

Staff who wish to remain in the positions they had during the previous year should be given first choice, contingent upon a positive work evaluation. New staff are assigned to vacancies within the program. Positions in a school should be filled in the same manner as they are in a business—by the people who would best perform the job.

Position assignments of previous year employees are made according to request. Notices such as the one shown in Figure 67 should be filled out by the employees prior to the end of each school year.

Notification of Staff Changes

If staff changes occur during the school year a letter should go to the parents of the children in those classes. The letter should state the new staff member's name and his/her credentials. There should be an introduction by the director and the school board, and a statement from the new staff member. This letter should be developed and sent before the new employee starts the job. Parents must always be notified of personnel changes in their child's class. This makes for easier transition for the children and develops trust between parents and the school.

Staff Orientation

Staff orientation was discussed in Chapter Six. This section is concerned only with new staff orientation, which should take place prior to the first regular staff meeting of the year. This meeting should be used to acquaint new staff members with the policies and procedures of the school, their room

ABC Preschool

Dear Staff,

As in the past, this year's contracts will expire at the end of the school year. Next year's contracts will be effective from August to May.

Please complete the bottom of this form and return by _____. At the end of the school year all positions are considered vacant, with the exception of the director. After completion of interviews, new contracts will be offered and signed.

Positions will be filled according to the availability of classes.

If you have any questions, please come see me.

Thanks,

Director

Name: _____

Position Preference: _____

    1st Choice: _____

    2nd Choice: _____

    3rd Choice: _____

Time: _____ Days: _____

Comments: _____

_____

_____   _____
    Signature   Date

Figure 67. Example of notice to staff.

assignments, benefit programs, tax and insurance information, and services and supplies offered by the school. This meeting (with the director) should be approximately one hour in length, giving ample time for presentation of materials, questions, and discussion. This needs to be an informal meeting, so new members feel at "home" with the school. After this meeting new staff should be given ample time to review material and equipment within their classrooms.

Staff Meetings

Regular staff meetings are a must for a good program. Meetings should be held once a month on a regular day, e.g., the second Friday of each month at 1:00 P.M. These meetings provide the staff with stability, an opportunity to review procedures, air grievances, develop friendships, share ideas, discuss problems, build self-confidence, receive pertinent information from the director and board, discuss parent or volunteer programs, and so on. Make these meetings informative, fun, and as brief as possible.

Tax Information

Each staff member should complete a W-4 form to be placed in his/her file. Also, a payroll sheet should be prepared for each employee. Each employee's tax records must also be kept up to date. Employees are required to notify the director or bookkeeper immediately of changes in their tax status. During the month of January (before January 30) each employee must be given a completed W-2 form to be filed with their tax returns. It is the employer's responsibility to provide accurate tax forms to the employee and to retain and file accurate tax records.

Insurance

The school board should decide what (if any) insurance coverage the program will provide for the employees. Some pro-

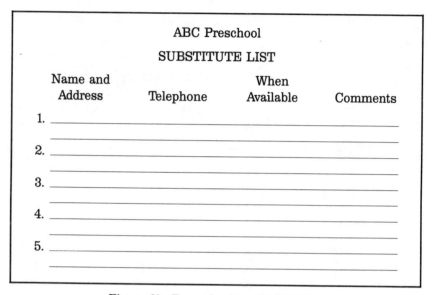

Figure 68. Example of a substitute list.

grams do not provide medical insurance because the employee's spouse insurance covers him/her. However, such a policy violates equal employment protection and is typically considered gender biased. The school board should develop an insurance policy that is consistent and equitable for all employees.

Substitutes

The director should keep a list of persons interested in substituting for preschool personnel, as shown in Figure 68. These people can be parents of children enrolled, former employees, friends of staff members, etc. Persons on this substitute list should be reliable and able to work on short notice. The director should keep a time sheet for each substitute with the date and hours worked, and the names of staff members they substituted for.

A substitute pay scale should also be developed. Some schools have different rates of substitute pay for teachers and teaching assistants. Other schools have a basic rate of pay for substitutes regardless of whom they substitute for. Substitutes should be informed of this wage prior to their first day of work.

The director should determine who is responsible for calling a substitute. A method that works well is for the staff member to notify the director, who then calls the substitute. Another alternative is to ask the staff members to contact their own substitutes. Often part-time staff members will serve as substitutes for full-time employees.

Employee's Absentee Record

Each employee's file should contain a record of his/her absences, such as the one shown in Figure 69.

Policy and staff regulations should define when an absence will be paid or not paid. An example policy could give each employee one working week of paid sick leave per year (a working week consists of the total number of hours spent in class time per week). Sick leave should be noncumulative. Excessive absenteeism (as determined by the school board) should be grounds for termination of a contract.

Staff Pay Periods

Each board will determine a pay schedule for the staff. If the program is twelve-month, pay periods can be monthly, bi-monthly, bi-weekly, or weekly. Since tuition generally is collected monthly, a pay period around the 10th or 15th of each month works well. This way if tuition is due the first of the month, the money is received prior to paying staff.

Name			
Date	Reason for Absence	Pay/No Pay	Substitute

Figure 69. Example of employee absence record.

ABC Preschool				
Year's Salary	Total for Summer	Twelve-Month	FICA Match	Hold Monthly (9)
$5484.96	$1469.28	$457.08	$32.68	$163.26

Figure 70. Example of employee pay.

A program that operates for nine months can give employees the option of being paid for nine or twelve months. Experience has shown that most employees prefer to be paid in twelve-month increments. This can be accomplished (in a nine-month program) by taking an employee's yearly salary and dividing it by twelve. The next step is to compute the tax on the salary, then add the gross amount plus the FICA matching funds for the summer months, divide this by nine and deposit this amount each month during the school year into a savings account. An example is shown in Figure 70.

The $163.26 should be deposited into a savings account each month during the school year. This system will give the employee the opportunity to have a smaller check during the school year, but during the summer they will receive the same salary while they are not working. The school board should formally adopt a policy on employee pay. An easier method for the school involves paying only during the school year (nine months).

Important: If you decide to pay over twelve months—the money that is being accumulated in the savings account should be used *only* for summer salaries. Do *not* use this for anything else. It is very important that you budget the money carefully for salaries.

Staff Evaluations

Evaluating all staff members is a must for an effective preschool program and should be done at least yearly. A staff member also needs to be provided the opportunity to evaluate the program, director, and other service areas that the school board deems necessary. We often think of staff evaluations as only evaluations of staff members, but the staff needs the opportunity to reciprocate. Figure 71 shows the sort of Program Evaluation that could be made available to staff members.

When the director evaluates the staff, he/she will need two copies of the evaluation form; one copy the director retains for the personnel files, and the other is for the staff member to retain. Most often the evaluation form should include a self-evaluation and an evaluation by the director. An example is shown in Figure 72.

ABC Preschool

PROGRAM EVALUATION

Please answer the following questions so that the program at ABC Preschool can be improved.

What improvements would you suggest to the director? _____
_____
_____

What positive aspects do you see in the director? _____
_____
_____

What do you like about the program? _____
_____
_____

If you could, what would you like to see changed? _____
_____
_____

Working conditions: _____
_____
_____

What are your overall feelings about your job at ABC? _____
_____
_____

Other Comments: _____
_____
_____

Figure 71. Example of a program evaluation form.

ABC Preschool

STAFF EVALUATION FORM

Name: _____   Date: _____

Never—N	Some—S	Usually—U
Most of the Time—M		Always—A

_____ 1. Have I imparted a positive feeling to others by arriving at school each day with an enthusiastic and cheerful attitude?

_____ 2. Have I always greeted my students in a friendly manner?

_____ 3. Have I accepted suggestions and constructive criticisms from other staff members gracefully?

_____ 4. Have I always remained flexible in my relationships with other adults (staff and parents)?

_____ 5. Have I always remained flexible in my relationships with my students?

_____ 6. Have I been able to retain my composure in tense situations?

_____ 7. Have I attempted to improve my skills in recognizing the needs of children on an individual basis?

_____ 8. Have I been aware of the sensitivities of my students?

_____ 9. Have I been tactful with my students?

_____ 10. Have I helped each child to develop friendships?

_____ 11. Have I helped each child to recognize his/her role as a member of a larger group?

_____ 12. Have I been realistic in the demands I have made of my students?

_____ 13. Have I made an effort to expand my knowledge of good early childhood teaching techniques?

_____ 14. Have I coordinated long-term and short-term goals for the overall improvement of my class program?

_____ 15. Have I been able to retain an overview of the class situ-

Figure 72. Example of a staff evaluation form.

ation rather than allow myself to get bogged down in petty details?

_____ 16. Have I developed warm relationships with parents of my students?

_____ 17. Have I made a conscious effort to remind myself of the developmental stage of each student?

_____ 18. Have I fostered independence in my students?

_____ 19. Have I maintained a child-oriented classroom?

_____ 20. Have I been conscientious in my daily attendance and the use of my sick leave?

_____ 21. Have I been loyal to the school and its philosophy?

_____ 22. Have I been loyal to the director of the school?

_____ 23. Have I avoided indulging in gossip about other staff members or about the families of my students?

_____ 24. Have I maintained professional attitudes in my demeanor and my personal relationships while on the job?

_____ 25. Have I assumed my share of joint responsibilities?

_____ 26. Have I displayed a willingness to participate in pertinent school activities outside of my regular hours?

_____ 27. Have I recognized my class as part of a unified school by avoiding possessiveness of my "own" group?

_____ 28. Have I carried positive and professional attitudes about the school into my community activities?

_____ 29. Have I loved each child without showing bias?

_____ 30. Have I maintained professional attitudes in all areas of my relationships with children, parents, and staff?

Summary of Evaluation: _____

_____

_____

Date: _____

Teacher's Signature: _____

Director's Signature: _____

Figure 72 (continued). Example of a staff evaluation form.

After completion of the evaluation forms, a conference should be scheduled for the staff member and director to discuss the form together. During the conference there should be sufficient time allotted for discussion and questions regarding the ratings each person has given on the evaluation forms. Remember that the primary reason for evaluation is to help the staff members recognize their strengths and their weaknesses, and to help them build on those strengths to become better.

A summary of the evaluation is completed (by the director) in duplicate. The director and employee sign and date both forms. Signing the form does not signify that the employee necessarily agrees with the evaluation, only that the teacher had an opportunity to view the evaluation and discuss it with the director. If there is dissatisfaction by the employee at his/her evaluation, it is the responsibility of the director to work with the employee to help him/her understand and correct the problems. If the employee cannot work with the director, he/she can request a conference with the director and the school board. This request needs to be in writing, and should be submitted to the director two weeks prior to the next scheduled board meeting.

The director's evaluation must be based on observation of a teacher's performance in the classroom. This formal evaluation should be done at least once per year, but experience indicates that a director should be in each classroom daily. One formal observation a year does not give an overall view of what a teacher is doing in the classroom. Also, it is the director's responsibility to know what is going on daily within the classrooms of the school. A sample observation chart is shown in Figure 73.

Each teacher is given a copy of the observation instrument. This observation form is discussed with the teacher immediately after the observation. All evaluations are confidential between the staff member and the director. Never discuss another staff member's observation/evaluation with anyone.

When areas of concern are discussed with staff members, the director needs to be fair, honest, objective, confidential, and constructive. The director should also stand his/her ground, take time to evaluate the situation, listen to the staff mem-

ABC Preschool

CLASSROOM OBSERVATION

Name of Teacher: _____ Date:_____

Environment:	Yes	No	Comments
Child-oriented	___	___	_____
Safe	___	___	_____
Ease of mobility	___	___	_____

General: _____

_____

Learning Centers:	Yes	No	Comments
Developmentally appropriate	___	___	_____
Varied	___	___	_____
Well-planned	___	___	_____
Creative	___	___	_____

General: _____

_____

Equipment Appearance:	Yes	No	Comments
Child-oriented	___	___	_____
Use of dittos	___	___	_____
Eye-pleasing	___	___	_____
Age-development appropriate	___	___	_____
Creative	___	___	_____
Amount used	___	___	_____

General: _____

_____

(continued)

Figure 73. Example of a classroom observation chart.

Activities:	Yes	No	Comments
Age appropriate	___	___	_____
Safe	___	___	_____
Balance between:			
group-individual	___	___	_____
quiet-active	___	___	_____
Available choices	___	___	_____
Flexible	___	___	_____

General: _____

_____

_____

Child-Teacher Interaction:	Yes	No	Comments
Appropriate	___	___	_____
Responds to each child	___	___	_____
Prejudice seen	___	___	_____
Observes child	___	___	_____
Aware of each child	___	___	_____
Correct use of open			
or closed questions	___	___	_____
Inspires children	___	___	_____
Attentive to responses			
of child	___	___	_____
Allows child to imitate	___	___	_____
Initiates activities	___	___	_____
Stimulating	___	___	_____
Interaction with other			
adults	___	___	_____
Full attention to child			
and his/her needs	___	___	_____

General: _____

_____

_____

Figure 73 (continued). Example of a classroom observation chart.

Discipline:	Yes	No	Comments
Expectations clear (rules)	___	___	_____
Treats all children similarly	___	___	_____
Reacts to inappropriate behavior quickly	___	___	_____
Uses correct voice tone	___	___	_____
Does not yell	___	___	_____
Aware of problems	___	___	_____
Anticipates problems	___	___	_____
Uses correct measures consistently	___	___	_____
Avoids threats	___	___	_____
Uses time out appropriately	___	___	_____
Helps children solve their own problems	___	___	_____

General: _____

\
_____

Educational Technique:	Yes	No	Comments
Develops and understands goals	___	___	_____
Prepares constructive lesson plans	___	___	_____
Develops long-term and short-term plans	___	___	_____
Helps children understand goals of an activity	___	___	_____

General: _____

\
_____

Director's Summary: _____

\
_____

Teacher's Response: _____

\
_____

Figure 73 (continued). Example of a classroom observation chart.

ber's evaluation of the same situation, think before speaking, get all the facts, be open-minded, accept criticism, treat all staff members equally, and work problems out in a professional manner.

Staff Personnel File

The employee's personnel file folder should contain the following:

(1) Application or resume
(2) Letters of reference
(3) Health and tuberculosis records
(4) Absenteeism record (from previous years and current)
(5) Evaluation sheets (classroom observation and self-evaluations)
(6) Contract
(7) Rules and regulations sheet
(8) W-4 Form
(9) Employee information sheet, such as shown in Figure 74.

Employee personnel files must be kept in a locked file cabi-

ABC Preschool

EMPLOYEE INFORMATION SHEET

Name: _____
      (First)   (Middle)   (Last)

Address: _____

_____
      (City)   (State)   (Zip)

Phone: _____ _____
      (Home)   (Other)

College (graduated)   Degree   Date

_____

_____

Social Security Number: _____

Figure 74. Example of employee information sheet.

net. These files are confidential and must not be retained where they may be seen by persons other than those designated to see them—the director, bookkeeper, and school board members when seated as a board.

Problems with Staff

When problems arise within the staff, it is the duty of the director to respond. The director should investigate problems and have a confidential conference with staff member(s) to find ways to alleviate dissention. It is then the duty of the staff (per their regulations) to discuss the concerns and to consider viable solutions to the concerns and diligently work to react in a professional manner. Problems should be settled as quickly as possible for the good of all concerned, especially the school. If the problem(s) cannot be remedied through the director, they should be brought before the school board at the next scheduled meeting.

At times there may be a staff member the school does not wish to rehire. This person should be notified of the intention at the earliest possible date, preferably before April 15. The director should meet privately with this staff member to give notification of nonrenewal. The staff member should not be surprised by the decision if the director has developed an ongoing evaluation procedure and has maintained an honest relationship with the staff member.

Dismissal of an Employee

The following steps should be followed in the dismissal of an employee. Following these may prevent a future lawsuit from the employee being dismissed.

RULE ONE:

Be careful to document actual behavior. Every action must be written down. Document (write) specific incidents of rules infractions or behaviors, including:

(1) Date and time logged
(2) Who was involved
(3) Where the incident occurred
(4) Cause
(5) The infraction
(6) Statements from employee
(7) Statements from a witness

RULE TWO:

Keep every incident documented and in the employee's personnel file. Give the employee a copy of every document in his/her personnel file. A good rule of thumb is to ask yourself:

(1) Would I have overlooked this infraction in other employees?
(2) Would I have been as severe if another employee had done this?
(3) Am I prejudiced against this employee?

RULE THREE:

Have an evaluation conference with the employee, and be sure to do the following:

(1) Discuss the reasons for concern.
(2) Listen to the employee's explanation.
(3) Consider any mitigating circumstances.
(4) Determine whether the employee was aware of the infraction.
(5) Determine whether it was a violation of the job description.
(6) Let the employee know of your disapproval of their behavior and/or actions.
(7) Put employee on "notice," giving fair warning that repetition of the action may be grounds for dismissal.
(8) Document the conference, date, time, and locations. Write down the key points and particular events you feel may be relevant if the exact words were used in court.

(9) Suggest alternative actions and/or behaviors that will remediate the situation, and work closely with the employee to judge improvement.

(10) Ask the employee to sign the conference statement and provide them with a copy.

There must be sufficient and valid reasons for the decision not to rehire a staff member. Dismissal is very touchy legally. Remember to document accurately, be fair, follow correct procedure for dismissal, and not hinder the former staff member's search for new employment. Handle this situation legally and in a professional manner. It would be nice to report that employee dismissal will never occur, but sooner or later an employee will have to be dismissed. Be prepared to do it with accuracy and care.

Below are reasons for which there is sufficient cause to dismiss staff:

(1) Evaluation reports that consistently indicate that the employee is not suitable to work with preschool children

(2) Ineffectiveness in the classroom

(3) Employee has violated one or more of the regulations of the "Job Description" after being informed of a violation and after an effort was made by the director to assist the employee in improving performance

(4) Inability to communicate with parents

(5) Employee has discussed confidential matters concerning children or their parents and/or staff members with anyone who will listen

(6) Employee has been openly defiant to the director and violated policies in doing so

(7) Employee has given false information on employment application

(8) Addiction to alcohol and/or drugs—or use of either on school premises

(9) Employee has been convicted of child abuse

(10) Employee has been negligent in the supervision of children

In-Service Programs

In-service programs for staff should be varied and informative. The topics can be presented by the director, a guest speaker, another staff member, a videotape, or a movie. Programs can include workshops, visits to other schools, small group discussions, or working within large groups.

Topics should further the knowledge of the staff. A few topics that can be used are:

- first-aid
- CPR
- educational programs
- sexual abuse
- parent-staff relations
- interest centers
- circle time
- stress management
- legal points
- discipline
- cooking
- classroom technique
- bulletin boards
- importance of play in the classroom

There are many more topics—use the needs of the staff to determine the in-service topics.

Summer

Each teacher's summer address and phone number should be on file for mailing paychecks (if the school has chosen to use the twelve-month pay schedule), and for sending correspondence concerning orientation meetings. It is a good idea to have the staff plan individual or group get-togethers during the summer to keep in touch. Maintaining contact during vacation helps to develop close relationships between staff. These contacts remind everyone that there are friends and colleagues who care about them. It is strongly recommended that summer activities or contacts be a part of the program structure.

CHAPTER NINE

Health and Safety

HEALTH IS THE THING THAT MAKES YOU FEEL THAT NOW IS
THE BEST TIME OF THE YEAR.
> —Franklin Pierce Adams

A child's physical and emotional development are major parts of the preschool program. Children who are well-adjusted, both physically and mentally, should be the school's goal. It is important to note that all children do not fall into the norm category, and it is the job of the director to know where to go, and who to contact to enable the child to receive the help he/she needs to grow. Making a list of all the community agencies that provide services to young children will prepare the director for discussions with parents. This list will help give the parent some partial resources and solutions to their child's problem.

The most common developmental delay for children is speech. Locating a reputable Speech and Hearing Clinic and becoming acquainted with their staff and program is an excellent route to advising parents.

Some children may come to school with emotional problems; in this situation a reputable child psychologist needs to be contacted. However, remember that the school cannot have a child tested or evaluated without parental consent.

Helping the child must be a joint venture between the school and the parents. It is very difficult to face parents and inform them of a problem with a child. The preschool could ignore the problem and let the elementary school handle it, but the time wasted would only harm the child. Recognizing and treating the problem at an early stage will give the child a much better chance of overcoming a problem. It is the duty of the preschool staff to make life as pleasant as possible for every child, helping them through problems that arise in their lives. Parents need to be informed of the school's concern. Guidance and en-

161

couragement will help parents follow through with the correct program. Many parents find it very difficult to face the fact that a child needs professional guidance, but with kindness, honesty, and true concern for the well-being of the child, the parents can feel assured that someone truly cares and wants to help. Some parents will react negatively to the suggestions for professional help. If this happens, the people involved (director, teacher, or teaching assistant) must feel that they've given it their best shot and accept the parents' wishes. Remember, the parents have the final choice. The school staff should help the child as much as possible through the program and keep the parents informed of the child's progress.

Handicapped Children

The school board will need to decide what procedure will be followed in enrolling handicapped children. This important issue should be included in the program pre-planning. The feasibility of enrollment, the staff needs, and the condition of the facility should be considered. Serving the handicapped child is an important area of early childhood education, and it is wise to predetermine a school policy.

Special Needs

Parents should make the preschool aware of any special health problems, such as allergies. A good solution to this problem is to include a section on the application that asks for allergies or other special needs.

Emergency Numbers and Policy for Action

Emergency telephone numbers and procedures should be included on the parent permission form. Parents need to be made aware by note, phone, or personal contact if a child has even a minor accident at school, as even the smallest bump on the head could result in a concussion. Informing parents of accidents will help the parent observe the child, and will show the program's concern for the child by this direct contact.

When an accident occurs, a teacher must fill out an accident report form and file it with the director. This form should be maintained in an accident report file and kept in the director's office for legal reasons. Figure 75 shows such an accident report form.

Communicable Diseases

Each year there will be chicken pox, lice, etc. Parents should be notified of the outbreak of the disease, its symptoms, incubation period, and the policy for returning children to school.

RETURN TO SCHOOL POLICY

The board should develop a policy concerning the procedure for children returning to school after illness, communicable disease, or lice. Check with the local health department for recommended guidelines. The most common childhood ailments, along with suggestions are listed below:

Chicken Pox–The child may not attend school until the last pimple has scabbed.

Cold–If there is a fever present the child may not attend school.

Diarrhea–The child may not attend school until the diarrhea has stopped.

Flu–If there is fever in the past twenty-four hours the child may not attend school.

Impetigo–A doctor's release should be required.

Lice–A doctor's release should be required.

Pink Eye–The child may not attend school until redness and discharge are gone. A doctor's release should be required.

Ringworm–The child may not attend school unless the spots are covered.

Scabies–A doctor's release should be required.

Scarlet Fever–The child may not attend school until forty-

```
┌─────────────────────────────────────────────────────────────┐
│                      ABC Preschool                          │
│                     ACCIDENT FORM                           │
│                                                             │
│  Name of Child: _____   │
│                                                             │
│  Date of Accident: _____  Time: _____    │
│                                                             │
│  Teacher: _____   │
│                                                             │
│  Parent Notification:                                       │
│      How: _____  Time: _____      │
│      Person Notified: _____   │
│                                                             │
│  Details of Accident: _____   │
│  _____    │
│  _____    │
│                                                             │
│  Procedures Taken: _____   │
│  _____    │
│  _____    │
│                                                             │
│  Results: _____   │
│  _____    │
│  _____    │
│                                                             │
│  Condition of Child: _____   │
│  _____    │
│                                                             │
│  Taken to the Hospital: _____ Yes _____ No              │
│                                                             │
│  Other Medical Procedures: _____   │
│  _____    │
│                                                             │
│  _____          _____       │
│  (Signature of Filing Teacher)             (Date)           │
│                                                             │
│  _____          _____       │
│  (Signature of Director)                   (Date)           │
└─────────────────────────────────────────────────────────────┘
```

Figure 75. Example of an accident report form.

eight hours after starting antibiotics. A doctor's release should be required.

Strep Throat—The child may not attend school until all soreness and symptoms are gone. This will take seven to ten days and a doctor's release is suggested.

Immunizations

In a preschool program it is not necessary to require health examinations or immunization certification unless the state in which the facility is located requires them. However, kindergarten children should be required to have these forms on file.

Medication at School

Because of various legal aspects, it is recommended that medication not be given to children while they are attending school.

Child Abuse

Each teacher and staff employee must be informed of how to observe child abuse and act responsibly. Law requires that suspected cases of child abuse be reported to proper authorities. As professionals, the primary responsibility of the school is to protect the child. The following are observable indicators of child abuse.

A child who is:

- frequently absent or late to school
- unclean or not appropriately dressed
- has frequent bruises, burns, or other injuries
- hyperactive, aggressive, disruptive, or destructive in behavior
- withdrawn, passive, and uncommunicative
- needs, but is not getting, medical attention

- undernourished
- tired
- tells of unusual parent behaviors

Professionals should also suspect a parent who is:

- aggressive or abusive
- habitually smelling of alcohol
- habitually unclean
- hostile to the teacher's questions concerning the child
- a known drug addict

Each state has different programs responsible for investigating a suspected case of child abuse. Be sure to check with state and local authorities for appropriate agencies.

First-Aid and CPR

Each staff member should have a knowledge of first-aid and CPR procedures. An inservice program designed to acquaint the staff with equipment and correct procedures is strongly suggested. Each school is required to have a first-aid kit on the premises.

Safety

The director must develop and maintain a safe environment for the children. Rules of safety need to be taught to the staff and children and continuously enforced. Facilities and equipment should be maintained to provide a safe environment. Repairs need to be made quickly on equipment, and unsafe areas or facilities need to be immediately upgraded.

The school board, director, and staff are liable if negligence is proven. The protection of children in the program, and visitors who enter the facility and grounds are of utmost concern. Below are some problem areas that could lead to negligence:

(1) Unsafe or defective equipment
(2) Defective building
(3) Improper or insufficient supervision of children

(4) Unsafe playground conditions

(5) Unsafe classroom or floor conditions

(6) Inadequate fencing

(7) Improper handrails for stairs

(8) Allowing a child to remain in school if the child's lack of self-control is dangerous to self and others

(9) Failure to provide a plan of building evacuation in case of fire or disaster

(10) Improper furnace or heating operation

(11) Improper or unsafe locks on doors and playground gates

(12) Failure to notify parents when a child is seriously ill or if the child has had an accident

(13) Use of improper information in obtaining health, fire, building safety, or other permits or licenses

(14) Unsanitary conditions

(15) Improper coverage of electrical outlets when not in use

Fire and Other Drills

An evacuation route must be established for each classroom in case of fire. A plan is also required for tornado drills. Remember, children should be taught the procedure for their protection so they can react promptly in an emergency. In tornado drills children file out of the room to an inner hallway or wall. They then squat down facing a wall and bend over with their face almost touching their knees and with hands over their head. This procedure scares children at first, but with practice they will adjust to the drill. Earthquake preparedness should also be practiced with children as a safety rule. Check with the local civil defense office for the correct procedures in each area.

Safety Rules

Children should be taught about the common dangers that surround them. A few of these are:

• safety with scissors and sharp objects

- keeping small objects, sharp objects, and other such items out of a child's mouth, ears, nose, and eyes
- proper use of playground equipment
- keeping chair legs on the floor
- climbing
- crossing streets
- running inside the building
- electrical outlets
- matches

Safety Education

A valuable part of each program is safety education. This program should include, but not be limited to, the following:

- safety kids
- tricycle and riding toy safety
- dealing with strangers
- seat belts (these should always be required on field trips)
- home safety
- toys and safety
- Officer Friendly and McGruff
- playground safety

CHAPTER TEN

School-Community Relations

WHAT WE'VE GOT TO DO IS TO KEEP UP OUR SPIRITS,
AND BE NEIGHBORLY.
WE SHALL COME ALL RIGHT IN THE END, NEVER FEAR.
—Charles Dickens

TODAY few mothers have the opportunity to stay at home with their young children. Financially, many mothers have had to reenter the work force in order to maintain a satisfactory standard of living for their family. Almost half of our nation's mothers are working outside the home. Grandparents are increasingly caring for the grandchildren as guardians. Parents of today are very mobile, thus breaking down the traditional extended family circle. There are many single parents, whether father or mother, and there are many multiple-sibling families. The standard American family of four—father, mother, and two children—is suffering under the increased pressures of our modern society.

Any new preschool program should consider the makeup of local parent structures. By realizing parent types, the program can meet the needs of those served. The school can play a vital role through parent programs by offering an excellent program for the preschoolers.

Parents want knowledge, help, reassurance, and a caring listener. Parents want to know that they are providing the stimulus their child needs to learn and grow. Parents want to understand that their feelings are shared by others. Most importantly, they want their child to grow and develop fully. In this everchanging age the preschool can be a parent's stability and friend. Plan parent communication well, so parents can feel safe and secure with the program they have chosen for their child.

Parents want to be assured that they are always welcome to visit the school unannounced. Parents of children enrolled in the preschool program should not have to make an appointment. Each program should have an "open-door" policy with parents. This policy means parents are welcome to visit the school at any time without prior notice. Parents may question what is really taking place in the school if they have to make an appointment to visit.

Communication

One of the basic tools needed by the director of the preschool is effective means of communication. Communications with parents should be truthful, pleasant, and helpful. Never "cut short" a parent. Remember, parents worry about their own child, not the others in the school. Questions may be asked a hundred times, but react as if each time is the first. Give parents the respect of full attention and take time to listen to their problems and concerns. If you cannot answer their questions, tell them you will examine the situation and always respond to each request for information.

Telephone

The admonition to smile when talking on the phone may sound silly, but it works. This skill alone conveys to the other party a pleasant and positive manner. Positive telephone manners are important to the efficient operation of the preschool, particularly with parents.

Correspondence-Enrollment Letters

Enrollment letters should be informative, pleasant, enthusiastic, and warm. This first contact with the school should make a parent feel welcome and enthusiastic about the program. Neatness is of vital importance in this initial contact with new parents. The initial perception is often the one that lasts when dealing with parents.

Pre-Registration Visits to School

A parent and child should feel that they are very important when they visit the school. The director and staff should be pleasant, helpful, enthusiastic, and warm to help transmit the feeling. The first impression of the school and staff is most important. All staff members should practice a positive attitude to help children and parents who want to enter the program. Take time to answer the parent's questions and be as well-organized as possible during this period of time. Parents want to see the director in charge.

Teacher Notes to Parents

Teacher notes to parents must be neat and to the point while depicting warmth and an attitude of caring. Even the simplest note concerning an event should be well-written and informative.

Newsletter

A monthly newsletter is an excellent way to facilitate open lines of communication between parents and the school. A letter from the director should be included in the newsletter, giving important dates, information, and events. Each teacher should also supply a letter including news and events about their classes. Figure 76 shows a sample newsletter.

Conferences

Parent-teacher conferences should be held at least twice a year. A good schedule would be to have the first conference prior to Thanksgiving and the second at the end of February. A conference should last between ten and twenty minutes, and

ABC Preschool

KID KHATTER

February 1990

Dear Parents,

We have really had bad weather since Christmas, let's hope that the snow and cold are now over. Information on snow days will come later.

There are several important dates in February that you should remember:

February 1—Tuition due
February 14—Valentine parties
            Be sure to check with your child's
            teacher about sending treats
February 20—Parent-Teacher conferences

As always, if you need to talk to me about anything, feel free to come to school or call.

Sincerely,

Director

Three Year Old News

(Put teacher's name here)

During January we have continued to work on the recognition of printed names, colors, numbers, the alphabet, and shapes. Much of our art work has stressed recognition of the four basic shapes (circle, rectangle, square, and triangle).

Your child has brought home papers on which he/she has printed (with our help, in most cases). Do not become alarmed if your child is unable to print these letters, as these printing sessions are aimed mainly at developing better control of fine motor skills.

Please do not hesitate to call if you wish to discuss anything concerning your child.

(A letter from each teacher should be included.)

Figure 76. Example of a preschool newsletter.

the teacher should strive to schedule a time convenient for the parents (although this is not always possible). Letters such as that shown in Figure 77 will help with scheduling. Each program should try to have 100% parent participation, which can be accomplished by conducting telephone conferences for those parents who cannot possibly arrange a time to visit. Parent-teacher conferences will be more successful if parents realize their importance. At the conference, important teacher behaviors include:

- positive attitude
- listening carefully to parents
- presenting problems and concerns in a helpful manner (not accusing)
- being punctual
- being confidential—*never* discuss another child with a parent
- not advising—give several suggestions to the parent, teachers are not all-knowing
- never engaging in a quarrel with the parent
- always being tactful and pleasant, but honest
- ending with a summary of what the parent and teacher need to work on to help the child

Retention

There will be times when student retention will need to be discussed with parents. At such times provide parents with the reasons for retention by relating potential benefits to the child. Always relay to the parent that the purpose of retention is to help the child. Do not alarm the parents. If retention is being discussed at the spring conference, parents should have been notified at the fall conference that their child was experiencing some problems. Retention should never come as a surprise at the end of school. It is the job of the teacher to keep the parents informed. Progress reports and samples of the child's work will serve as guides during conferences and will lay the foundation for retention, if needed.

ABC Preschool

Child's Name _____

Dear Parents,

Below you will find your conference date and time. Please mark this on your calendar and plan to attend. Conferences are scheduled every fifteen minutes—please be prompt and limit your conference to the specified length of time. In doing so, you will insure everyone of their allotted time.

If for some reason you cannot attend at the time given, please call your child's teacher to arrange a time convenient for both. To insure a worthwhile conference:

a. Have questions you wish to ask in mind before your arrival.
b. Limit your conversation to your child's progress.
c. Be prompt.
d. Limit your time to the allotted fifteen minutes.
e. Please do not bring your children.

We are looking forward to discussing your child's progress. Mark the time and date on your calendar. See you then.

Sincerely,

Director

- -

Conference Date: _____

Conference Time: _____

Conference Schedule

Date: _____   Class: _____

Time	Parents
7:30	Mr. and Mrs. Smith
7:45	Mr. and Mrs. Jones
8:00	Mrs. Boone
8:15	Mr. Delaney
8:30	Mr. and Mrs. Calhoun
8:45	Mr. Land
9:00	Mr. and Mrs. Johnson

Figure 77. Example of a conference letter.

Volunteers

There are many areas within the program that could benefit from the use of parent volunteers. Again, because so many mothers work the volunteer program may not be large, but no matter the size, a parent volunteer program can be an asset to the preschool program. Parents need to be made aware that the teacher is the person authorized to be in charge of the room and is the one who sets the rules. Each teacher should schedule his/her volunteers. The following are recommended suggestions when using parent volunteers:

- If a child is upset by the parent being present in the room, give the parent a job that keeps him/her out of the room.
- Be tactful and punctual.
- *Never* gossip to others about children.
- Volunteers should not bring younger siblings to the school when they volunteer.

Parents can assist in many ways. They can share a craft, go on field trips, give an art lesson, etc. Most of the time we think of volunteers as being only mothers, but fathers can share their skills and hobbies at school too. Remember grandparents also.

RELEASING VOLUNTEERS

There are those rare times when a volunteer is not suitable, in manner or confidentiality, to remain in the classroom. Try to find an alternative position for the volunteer, but if this still doesn't work, the director should tactfully release him/her from the duties.

Evaluations

Parents should be given the opportunity to evaluate the program each year. Many good ideas for program improvements can come from these anonymous evaluations. A sample parent program evaluation is included in Chapter Seven.

Orientation

A before-school parent orientation program gives parents the opportunity to become acquainted with the director, the handbook, policies and procedures, the classroom, and the teachers. This personal meeting helps parents feel more secure and confident in contacting the school and becoming a part of the total program. This meeting opens the door for parents to build confidence in their child's teacher. It also gives the parent an opportunity to feel totally welcome within the school program.

Parent Meetings

Parent meetings should be held at least twice a year for the specified purpose of providing opportunities where parents can share ideas, discuss concerns, become more acquainted with the program and its purpose, or just have fun.

There are a variety of topics that can be presented and discussed in these meetings; some suggestions are:

- effective parenting
- discipline
- what to look for in developmental delays
- child rearing—three to six years
- to read or not to read—age four
- math and the preschool child
- where to go for help (agencies to help parents)
- evaluating the preschool child

Home Visits

A visit to every student's home would be ideal. Unfortunately, because of class size and teacher class load, it is generally impossible. If the size of the school permits, home visits are excellent. A home visit allows the teacher to see the child in his/her own environment. These visits also give the teacher the opportunity to talk socially with parents. This part of the program can be a valuable asset and should be included if at all possible.

Local Resources

Each program should be well aware of the surrounding community. The community should not be blocked out. In fact, at every available opportunity the community should be involved in the school. Get to know the community and work to get the community acquainted with the school and its programs.

Outside Visitors

Occasionally the program will have visitors that are unknown. The director should meet with these people to answer their questions and to provide necessary information. The director should immediately be made aware of visitors within the facility. The director is responsible for protecting everyone—children, staff, and visitors within the walls of the facility. Visitors should have a limited stay within the classroom and be courteous and inconspicuous, during visits that should be prearranged if possible.

Visitors from other schools are asked to make an appointment with the director. The main reason for this appointment is to allow time for the director to become acquainted with the visitors and their purpose.

Pre-Registration Visits

Parents on pre-registration visits may bring the child with them. Consequently, the director should meet with each parent and child. After this brief meeting the director can escort the parent to the desired class and teacher, make introductions, and allow time for the parent to meet with the teacher. The parents should meet with the director prior to leaving.

Students

College students may have assignments to visit preschool classrooms. These visits should be cleared through the director. The program should welcome these students to the classrooms because the students and the preschool program can benefit from the experience.

High school students can also be an asset to the program. These students usually come on class assignment or as part of an intern program. High school students generally come for observation, not to take an active role. They may help with art projects, read stories, work with individual students, etc. These students are not trained workers, so their tasks will need to be teacher-formed and directed. Sample guidelines are shown in Figure 78.

ABC Preschool

GUIDELINES FOR STUDENT VISITORS

- The director should review the reason the students are visiting the school and the institution's expectations while observing.
- The teacher and assistant are in charge of the class and of work assignments.
- Students are not to visit among each other while in class.
- No loafing is allowed.
- Do assigned work.
- Dress appropriately.
- Do not chew gum.
- Be punctual.
- The director will make classroom assignments.
- Children are not to be discussed outside the school.

Figure 78. Guidelines for student visitors.

EVALUATION

College and intern students will be evaluated by the assigned preschool teacher. The college will usually provide these evaluation forms for their students. The classroom teacher should return the evaluation directly to the college.

Know Your Community

When beginning a program, make a list of available resources and "things to do" that will be of value to the program. For example:

FIELD TRIPS

- post office
- fire station
- police station
- fast food restaurant
- museum
- doctor and dentist
- hospital

THINGS TO HEAR ABOUT

- visiting lecture
- craft lesson
- parent's job
- Officer Friendly
- parent's collection (rocks, trophies, etc.)
- symphony

Early Childhood Organizations

Staff members should be encouraged to become members of the local affiliate of an early childhood education organization and take an active part in professional organizations. These organizations have several meetings a year with workshops, in-service sharing of ideas, educational updates, etc. The staff can grow professionally through staff development activities as a result of membership in professional organizations.

Colleges

Staff should be encouraged to further their professional growth by auditing or taking college coursework for credit. Their knowledge can also be shared with other staff members at faculty meetings. If financially possible, payment for college coursework in early childhood education should be fully or partially reimbursed by the preschool program.

CHAPTER ELEVEN

Day-Care

> HOLD CHILDHOOD IN REVERENCE AND DO NOT BE IN ANY
> HURRY TO JUDGE IT FOR GOOD OR ILL.
> GIVE NATURE TIME TO WORK BEFORE YOU TAKE OVER HER
> TASKS, LEST YOU INTERFERE WITH HER METHOD.
> —Jean Jacques Rousseau

DAY-CARE is becoming a much needed program. Over half of today's mothers work, and these mothers want a safe, secure atmosphere for their children while they are away from them. Professionals are able to provide this atmosphere for young children by making day-care an extension of an existing preschool program. The time has come for early childhood educators to provide this much-needed service.

Pre-Planning

STATE INSPECTIONS

Fire Marshall

Before beginning full preparation for a day-care program, facilities should be inspected by the state fire marshall's office. Day-care and preschool have the same space regulations for children: thirty-five square feet inside, and seventy-five square feet outside per child. However, fire regulations are stricter for day-care programs. Flame spread rating for walls, doors, and floor covering will need to be documented and filed with the state fire marshall's office. States differ in the required rating, so each state's regulations should be checked through the appropriate state office.

All doors in a day-care building must open out, and some states require automatic door closures on each door. Windows must allow exit from a room, and there must be a window exit in each classroom. Some states require only smoke alarms, while others require elaborate fire alarm systems with emergency exit lights. Fire extinguishers are required for both preschool and day-care programs, but the types and sizes may differ. Again, check with the appropriate state office.

Health Department

A local representative of the state health department will need to be contacted at the same time as the fire marshall. This department inspects bathrooms, kitchen areas, and the entire facility for health regulations.

Bathroom facilities wil be required to meet minimum standards of one commode and wash basin for each twenty children. Toilet facilities must be cleaned and sanitized daily. Separate toilet facilities must be provided for males and females. If possible, toilet facilities, especially wash basins, should be hung at child height.

Kitchen areas must be clean and equipped for proper food preservation, storage, preparation, and serving. Foods or supplies may not be stored in the same cabinet as janitorial supplies. Refrigerators must have a thermometer in both freezer and refrigerator compartments. Health department personnel will check the temperature of both areas as well as the storage area for dry foods.

STATE LICENSING AGENCY–DEPARTMENT OF HUMAN RESOURCES

Preceding the fire marshall and health inspections, application to the state licensing agency for a day-care license is required. A representative from that agency will visit the planned center to acquaint personnel with licensing procedures. The inspector will tour the facility and give specific instructions on set-up and development of the program as per state regulations. After the initial visit, the day-care facility will be required to meet the state's day-care standards.

Before opening the center to receive children, the state agent will return when everything is in place to begin operation. The program, forms, and facility are to be exactly as they would be if children were present. At that time the inspector will approve or reject the school's readiness to open the day-care facility. Within two weeks of the program's opening, with children present, the agent will return to inspect the operation and determine if the program is operating within the approved plan. This agent will also return unannounced periodically throughout the year. The inspecting agent should be considered an advisor, but will make certain that state regulations are being followed. Remember, the agent is there for the protection of the children and the program. They are not "out to get you," but to ascertain that the operation is safe and running correctly.

APPLICATION FOR LICENSE

Application for a state license should be made at least six months prior to the planned opening date. Processing the license and assigning a field agent to the proposed day-care program takes time. The agent has many day-care programs to inspect, so be patient because he/she will have to work your program into an already hectic schedule. This is the reason for filing early, so be prepared.

FINANCIAL ANALYSIS

Start-Up Costs

A determination of equipment, supplies, renovations, etc., will be required before starting, and should be made early. Where will this funding originate? Facility needs may determine whether the program is feasible or not.

Income

After the facility's capacity is established, the "cost break" number can be determined. This is the number of full-time children the program will require to be financially feasible. A "per hour," "per day," and "per week" fee amount should be set. The determination should be made if the program will accept only full-time children, or if drop-ins and other part-time children will be allowed. Always keep in mind the "cost break" point; admitting too many drop-ins will damage the total program.

The director must also determine if the income per child is to be "guaranteed." This means that parents receive two weeks vacation and one week sick leave per year. The remainder of the weeks are "guaranteed" income. Whether or not the child attends the program, the parents pay full tuition for those weeks. An epidemic like "chicken pox" can be financially devastating to a program that does not have "guaranteed" income. For those programs with sufficient seed money to be drawn upon when enrollment is low, "guaranteed" income is not necessary. Many day-care programs are using the "guaranteed program" as a safeguard against financial instability.

The program may wish to charge an annual supply fee. In small programs the supply fee plus a registration fee helps stretch the budget. Supplies are very expensive, especially in day-care programs where more money will be needed because of the length of the daily program. Fund raisers can be used to supplement income. However, careful thought should be given concerning the impact on parents before considering this alternative.

Cost

Staff salaries for a day-care program follow the same rules as a preschool does. A salary schedule, workman's compensation, medical, liability, insurance provisions, and employment status will need to be determined. Refer to Chapter Eight for further information.

Insurance

Fire and liability insurance are required before a program opens. Liability insurance should provide from $1 million to $5 million worth of protection. A School Accident Policy for the number of children and the staff involved in the program should be purchased. This type of policy covers the child/staff while they are at school and will pay benefits for accidental injury while on the premises, traveling to and from the premises, and while on field trips. This type of policy can be purchased for nine or twelve months at a cost of approximately $4.50 per person (child or staff).

FOOD SUPPLIES

The day-care program will often be required to provide a daily breakfast, morning snack, lunch, and afternoon snack. (Some programs do not provide breakfast.) The cost for food items should be determined during the planning procedure. Food does not have to be elaborate, but must be nutritious and well-balanced. A commercial food service can be contracted to provide the lunch meal. The service can prepare the meal and deliver it hot and ready to serve. They provide plates, cups, drinks, and utensils (all plastic) for approximately $1.00 per serving. This service will eliminate hiring a cook or other food personnel. Concern for storage, food preparation, drinks, and dinnerware will be removed from the director. A staff member will usually be responsible for cleaning scraps and rinsing out containers for the service to pick up the following day. However, the state must approve the use of a food service.

Another alternative is to contract with a local public school's lunchroom to buy enough meals for the program. Check this option because it could substantially reduce start-up costs and future operating costs. Sample menus and program count forms are given in Figures 79 and 80, respectively.

CONSUMABLES

Consumables include paper and other nonreusable supplies whether for the classroom, office, or for cleaning use. The cost of these items should be budgeted on a yearly basis. A supply fee can help defray the costs for consumables.

CLEANING, RENT, AND UTILITIES

Who is responsible for cleaning, rent, and utilities? Cleaning can be professionally contracted, or a custodian may be hired. The day-care area needs to be cleaned and sanitized daily.

Rent is sometimes charged for using the area. If the day-care is an outreach for another program, rent will often not be

ABC Day-Care

MENU PLANNING FORM

Week of: _____

MEAL PATTERNS

BREAKFAST
Juice or fruit and/or cereal
Milk

A.M. SNACK
Milk, juice, fruit, or vegetable
Bread or cereal

NOON MEAL
Meat and/or alternate
Vegetables and/or fruits
Bread
Milk
Other foods

P.M. SNACK
Milk, juice, fruit, or vegetable
Bread or cereal

EVENING MEAL
Meat and/or alternate
Vegetables and/or fruits
Bread
Milk

Figure 79. Example of menu planning form.

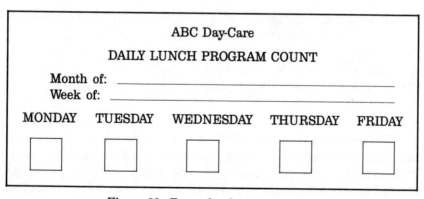

ABC Day-Care

DAILY LUNCH PROGRAM COUNT

Month of: _____
Week of: _____

MONDAY	TUESDAY	WEDNESDAY	THURSDAY	FRIDAY

Figure 80. Example of program count.

charged. However, for private day-care programs, rent and utilities will be the two largest expenses other than staff costs. Try to obtain an inexpensive rental property that fulfills the requirements of the program. The appearance and location of the facility will be the primary determiners for parent participation.

More public schools, churches, and businesses are becoming interested in day-care programs for their employees and/or clientele. The local chamber of commerce could have information on the larger employers and churches in the area. Contact with these prospects could assist in locating reasonable facilities and a "ready market" of potential students.

Many utility companies are now "cost averaging" utility bills to reduce the fluctuation of monthly statements. The cost averaging could be a real advantage to a beginning program or one that is marginally stable. Check with local utility companies for full details.

DIRECTOR

The preschool job description for program director may also be used in day-care for this position. The director should be contracted near the beginning of the planning process so he/she will be able to meet with the state agencies in setting up the program. His/her suggested hours are 8:00 A.M.–4:30 P.M. The director does not need to be at the center during the entire hours of operation. A designated staff member can handle the opening and closing of the center. However, the director should be hired on a twelve-month basis.

PROJECTION OF ENROLLMENT

The age of children in the day-care program ranges from infant to six years. After school care students can range in age from six years to twelve years. Staff members are added in proportion to the number of children that the facility serves. A market feasibility study can and should be conducted to verify this projection.

Preparation

STAFF

Staff regulations, contracts, tax information, orientation, etc., are basically the same as for the preschool. Working hours will be different and so will the staff-child ratios. Day-care staff will be required to record their arrival and departure times. Some sample documents relating to day-care startup are given in Figures 81–87.

Orientation

Parent orientation for the day-care program should be similar to that used for preschool. The major difference is the loading and unloading procedure. Day-care parents are required to accompany children to and from the building, and to sign the children in and out of the center. A parent orientation meeting should be scheduled to familiarize parents with the procedures, regulations, staff, and rooms. Allow ample time for discussion. Further details can be found in Chapter Six.

Costs and Fees

COST

The school board, in its consideration of fees, will need to determine if families with more than one child will receive "cost breaks." Many day-care facilities give a 20% discount for additional children. Procedures concerning sick days, vacation (of parents), and summer school will also need to be decided and should be given consideration at an early stage in the planning process.

PAYMENT

The student registration fee should be due with the student application and should be nonrefundable. Supply fees (if charged) should be due before the first day of class. Weekly payments should be due each Friday when the parent picks up the child (unless arrangements have been made with the director). If there are separate charges for lunches, they should be paid on Friday with weekly tuition.

DELINQUENT ACCOUNTS

Accounts must be paid in full each week, or the child should not be admitted on the following Monday. Refer to the Parent Handbook in Appendix B.

ABC Day-Care

September 10, 1990
Dear Staff,

By now you think that I've forgotten, but really I have not. We have had several delays with the building, but everything seems to be going smoothly now and I can give you some definite dates. Please mark the following on your calendar:

(1) Staff meeting: Monday, September 24th at 9:00 A.M.
(2) Tuesday, September 25th: Parent Orientation Meeting, 7:30 P.M. in the main building.
(3) Thursday, September 27th: Children's Open House, 7:00–8:00 P.M.
(4) October 1st: School opens

Please remember, I need your tuberculosis skin test report before the staff meeting.

I'm sure you are as anxious to get started as I am. I look forward to the opportunity to work with you this year.

See you September 24th.

Sincerely,

Day-Care Director

P.S. Teachers, you have $100.00 for supplies to begin the year. Turn in your requested supply list at the staff meeting.

Figure 81. *Example of an orientation meeting letter (on letterhead).*

ABC Day-Care
(should be posted on the bulletin board)

I. General Regulations
  A. A file box will be provided to each class for work that needs to be copied.
    1. When work is completed, it will be returned to your box.
    2. Please put a note on work to be done, stating the number of copies and date needed.
  B. A sign-in sheet will be on the bulletin board for children. A parent *must* sign the child in and out each day, stating the exact time for arrival and departure.
  C. Rest mats will be stored in the playroom after nap time. Children's sheets, etc., are to be sent home each Friday to be laundered.
  D. Each child must have his/her own cubby.
    1. On Friday, each cubby must be wiped out by a staff member.
  E. Parents may visit unannounced as often as they wish.
  F. Every staff member is required to report any sign of parent-child abuse to the director immediately.
  G. All kitchen doors are to be kept closed at all times.
  H. Children must be served daily:
    1. Morning snack
    2. Lunch
    3. Afternoon snack
  I. *No* field trips in cars, buses, etc., will be allowed.
  J. Neighborhood walks will be allowed.
  K. When painting, children are to wear smocks and the floors must be protected.
  L. Children must not use the kitchen as a throughway.

II. Staff Regulations
  A. Hours and salaries:
    1. Each staff member must be in his/her room fifteen minutes prior to shift.
    2. Each staff member must sign in and out on the time sheet, stating exact times of arrival and departure.
      a. When late for any reason, a staff member must contact the director at least one hour before his/her shift begins, if at all possible.

Figure 82. Example of day-care regulations.

b. Unnecessary tardiness:
   (1) Pay will be withheld.
   (2) Five occurrences will constitute grounds for dismissal.
3. Salaries are not paid when school is not in session.
4. Sick day provisions:
   a. Contact director as soon as possible.
   b. One contract week of sick days are paid. If additional days are taken, pay will be withheld.
5. All staff members are paid on an hourly pay scale.

B. General staff regulations:
1. Accident reports are to be filled out and turned in to the director immediately.
2. Fire drills will be held monthly. Tornado drills will also be held monthly. Proper records will be maintained on all drills stating time, date, and number of children involved.
3. Teachers are to turn in a monthly lesson plan by the last full week of the preceding month.
   a. The program will be geared to the needs of the individual child with concerns for his/her interests, handicaps, special talents, and individual style and pace of learning.
4. Staff will act professionally toward parents and other staff members.
   a. Staff will plan and implement methods of establishing a positive liaison with parents.
5. *No smoking* is allowed at any time in the building.
6. Child discipline:
   a. Children will be treated in a patient manner.
   b. Physical, mental, emotional, or sexual abuse of a child in any manner will constitute grounds for immediate dismissal of staff member.
   c. All staff abuse incidents will be reported to the police and the social worker.
   d. Any problems with children are to be discussed with the director. The child's parent will be contacted by the director. A conference will be set up for the director and teacher to meet with the parent.
   e. If a satisfactory arrangement cannot be reached, parents will be given written notification that their child must be removed from the school within five school days following notification.

(continued)

Figure 82 (continued). *Example of day-care regulations.*

8. Playground times will be scheduled by the teachers. Each teacher will be responsible for making sure that the playground is free of debris, and is safe for the children.
9. At least one staff member will be with the children at *all* times (including the rest room). Do not leave the children *unattended* at any time for any reason.
10. Supplies:
    a. These will be kept in each individual classroom.
    b. These will be ordered by the director, unless otherwise specified.
11. Staff members are not to take payments on day-care accounts. Payments are to be taken by the director or secretary only. An envelope for payment will be attached to the bulletin board. If the director and secretary are unavailable, the parent may place payment in the envelope. A receipt should be issued for all money received.
12. Staff and/or parent problems:
    a. By order of the school board:
       (1) The director shall have authority over any problems arising between staff members.
       (2) The director shall be notified immediately of any problems arising between staff members.
           (a) If a satisfactory solution cannot be reached, the staff member involved will be granted due process which may culminate in a meeting with the school board.
           (b) Staff members (including director and secretary) will abide by the final decision of the school board in all personnel matters.
13. Staff meetings will be held each month and will include staff development activities.
14. Teachers are to be sure the room is cleaned before leaving, including:
    a. Run the sweeper each day.
    b. Take out trash each day.
15. Alcohol and illegal drugs are prohibited on the premises.
16. Each staff member will carry out the responsibility and duties specified in his/her contract. Salary will be specified in each employee contract.

Figure 82 (continued). Example of day-care regulations.

C. Individual staff member responsibilities:
  1. Persons having authority over the day-care will be:
     a. The director, in his/her absence
     b. The secretary, when both the director and secretary are absent
     c. The designated staff member
        (1) Early assistant will be responsible until the designated teacher arrives.
        (2) Late assistant will be responsible after the designated teacher's departure, until closing.
  2. Early assistant will:
     a. Have the authority of day-care until the director, secretary, or designated teacher arrives.
     b. Unlock the school and turn on lights.
     c. Check bathrooms for supplies.
     d. Make sure all children are properly signed in by parent.
     e. Observe children for health problems.
     f. Keep early arrivals in playroom until class time, in an orderly manner.
     g. Pick up lunches.
     h. Make sure the kitchen is clean before the end of his/her shift.
  3. Designated teacher will:
     a. Be responsible any time the director and secretary are out of the day-care building.
     b. When state official comes in, he/she will send someone to summon the director and/or secretary (if one or the other is out of the building).
  4. Late assistant will:
     a. Stay until the building is clear of all children.
     b. Make sure center is clean and orderly before leaving.
     c. Make sure bathrooms have been disinfected.
     d. Make sure parents sign out children.
     e. Report late (after 5:30 P.M.) parent arrival to the director immediately and keep time of late arrival.
     f. Turn out lights.
     g. Make sure that the playground gate is locked.
     h. Close the school and make sure all the outside doors are locked.

Figure 82 (continued). Example of day-care regulations.

ABC Day-Care

PERSONS HAVING AUTHORITY OVER
THE DAY-CARE WILL BE

(1) The director, in his/her absence
(2) The secretary, when both the director and secretary are absent
(3) The designated staff member
(4) Early assistant will be responsible until designated teacher arrives
(5) Late assistant will be responsible after designated teacher's departure, until closing

Figure 83. Example of authority ranking.

ABC Day-Care

PERSONS TO CONTACT CONCERNING DAY-CARE

(Please contact in the following order)

Name	Phone Number
(1) Director	111-1111
(2) Secretary	222-2222
(3) Attorney	333-3333
(4) School Board President	444-4444

Figure 84. Example of contact list.

ABC Day-Care

STAFF TIME SHEET

Staff Member: _____

Week of: _____

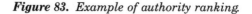

Monday		Tuesday		Wednesday		Thursday		Friday	
IN	OUT	IN	OUT	IN	OUT	IN	OUT	IN	OUT

Substitutes: _____

Figure 85. Example of a staff time sheet.

ABC Day-Care

STAFF TRAINING AND DEVELOPMENT MEETING

Agenda for: (Date) _____

(1) Turn in second semester supply list, also any daily supplies, snacks, etc., you may need.

(2) Report any child's illness during school hours to either the director or secretary, we will contact parent.

(3) We need the exact count of children in each class.

(4) Be sure to put a copy of any individual class note sent home, in the director's office.

(5) C.P.R. classes will be held on October 15th, 16th, and 17th, from 6:30 P.M.–9:30 P.M.

(6) Newsletter articles and monthly class plans for October are due by September 24th.

(7) Staff meetings will be held this year on the first and third Thursday of each month.

(8) Other staff concerns.

Initialed by: _____

Figure 86. Example of staff meeting notice and agenda.

ABC Day-Care

Open   7:15 A.M.–3:15 P.M.
       7:30 A.M.–3:30 P.M.
       7:45 A.M.–3:45 P.M.
       8:00 A.M.–5:00 P.M.

Close   3:30 P.M.–5:30 P.M.

Figure 87. Example of staff work schedule.

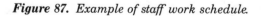

195

ADDITIONAL FEES

Additional fees should be charged for children remaining in the center after 5:30 P.M., or whatever the official closing time is for the day-care program, if the parent does not telephone prior to 5:15 P.M. Keeping the center open necessitates paying staff and often means increased utility costs.

Forms

A number of commonly used forms are shown in Figures 88–95. Completed registration applications should be required for admission to the day-care program. Included with the application should be a permission form and a doctor's form. These forms should be required before a child can be admitted to the program. For more detailed information refer to Chapter Six.

Payment

Some parents may wish to pay their account monthly. This can be done without any additional problems to most book-keeping procedures. (NOTE: Make sure they pay every month because day-care tuition is accrued weekly and a balance can be several hundred dollars if the account goes longer than a month.) Enforce the payment policy so that parents do not get behind in payments. A record of payment such as the one in Figure 96 can be sent to each parent to help them file their tax returns, a policy that parents really appreciate.

Medical

Other than the physician's form, which must be on file before a child's entrance to the program, there will be letters informing parents of communicable diseases, lice, impetigo, and other infections that are present in the school. Figure 97 is an example of a letter that would be appropriate to send parents informing them of possible chicken pox infection.

ABC Preschool and Day-Care

July 9, 1990
Dear Parents,

As you know, ABC Preschool is starting its ninth year of operation. Throughout those years, we have often been asked to develop a program of day-care so that working mothers could bring their children in the morning and leave them until the work day is over. Because of space limitations, we have been unable to offer such a program until this time.

This year we are developing a day-care program and will offer full day-care for your child, if you need the service.

The day-care program will include morning preschool class, with after school care until 5:30 P.M. The cost of the program will be $45.00 per week and will begin on August 20th.

The day-care program will be a twelve-month session for children ages three years and up. We will also offer elementary children an after school program during the school year, and an all-day summer program.

If you, or someone you know, would like to enroll in this program, please contact me as soon as possible to reserve a place for your child, since we will be limited as to the number of children we can serve.

Sincerely,

Director

Figure 88. *Example of a recruitment letter.*

ABC Preschool and Day-Care

July 30, 1990
Dear Parents,

We thank you for your interest in the ABC Preschool Day-Care program. It is our purpose to provide your child not only with day-care while you work, but with a five-day preschool readiness program, as we do with our existing preschool. We believe that children ages three, four, and five years old can benefit from a preschool experience throughout their formal education. A good beginning sets the pattern for a constructive formal education. For these reasons we are incorporating the preschool curriculum in the day-care program.

We intend to open the day-care program no later than September 17th, and hopefully by August 20th. We realize, with school starting soon, the August 20th date would be more convenient for everyone, but we must wait until the Department of Human Resources allows us to open. We hope you will be patient. In the meantime, we will try our best to get the Department of Human Resources to hurry their work.

Enclosed you will find the following:

(1) Day-care enrollment application
(2) Pre-admission report (to be completed by your physician)
(3) Day-care information booklet (all fees and policies of the program are included in the booklet)

When completing these forms, please keep in mind that the questions we have asked are for the purpose of helping us to protect, care for, and give appropriate guidance to the child you are entrusting to us. There will be a parent orientation meeting prior to the day-care opening. We will let you know the date as soon as possible.

Again, thank you for your interest in our new program. If you have any questions, please do not hesitate to call.

Sincerely,

Director

Figure 89. Example of a pre-enrollment letter.

ABC Preschool and Day-Care

APPLICATION FOR ENROLLMENT IN DAY-CARE
Registration Fee: $35.00 (nonrefundable)

CIRCLE PROGRAM DESIRED:

(1) Full Day: 7:30 A.M.–5:30 P.M.
(2) Kindergarten/Pre-kindergarten Class:
    day-care hours 11:00 A.M.–5:30 P.M.
(3) After School Program (elementary) 2:30 P.M.–5:30 P.M.

Child's name:_____
         (Last)   (First)   (Middle)   (Nickname)

Birthdate: _____   Home phone: _____
      (Month, Day, Year)

Address: _____
                (Street)

_____
(City)   (State and Zip)

Father's name _____
Place of employment _____ Work phone _____
Address _____
Mother's name _____
Place of employment _____ Work phone _____
Address _____
Marital status of parents:

____ Married   Stepfather _____
____ Separated   Stepmother _____
____ Divorced

Remarks _____

Custody/visiting arrangements _____

Names and ages of sisters/brothers _____
_____
_____

Child's physician _____ Phone _____
Church _____
Does the child have any special fears? _____
_____

What past illnesses has child had?
__ Scarlet Fever __Chicken Pox __ Mumps
__ Measles   __Other _____

(continued)

Figure 90. Example of a day-care application.

Does child have frequent colds? _____ yes _____ no

Frequent: __ Tonsillitis __ Mumps
           __ Stomach aches __ Other _____

Has he/she had any serious accidents? Explain.

_____

Is the child allergic? If so, how is it usually manifested?
__ Asthma   __ Hay Fever
__ Hives   __ Other _____

Has child ever been to a dentist? _____ yes _____ no

Has child had his/her vision tested? _____ yes _____ no

                    hearing tested? _____ yes _____ no

Date _____ Parents signature _____

Please add any comments you think would aid us in caring for
your child:

_____
_____
_____

Figure 90 (continued). Example of a day-care application.

ABC Preschool and Day-Care

PARENT PERMISSION FORM

I hereby grant permission for my child to use all of the play
equipment and to participate in all of the activities of the school.

I hereby grant permission for my child to leave the school
premises under the supervision of a staff member for neighborhood walks.

I hereby grant permission for my child to be included in evaluation and pictures connected with the school program.

I hereby grant permission for the director or acting director to
take whatever steps are necessary to obtain emergency medical
care, if warranted. These steps may include, but are not limited
to, the following:

(1) Attempt to contact a parent or guardian.
(2) Attempt to contact the child's physician.
(3) Attempt to contact you through any of the persons you list on
    this form.

Figure 91. Example of a permission form.

(4) If we cannot contact you or your child's physician we will do any or all of the following:
  a. Call another physician or the paramedics.
  b. Call an ambulance.
  c. Have the child taken to an emergency hospital in the company of a staff member.
(5) Any expenses incurred under (4) above, will be borne by the child's family.
(6) The school will not be responsible for anything that may happen as a result of false information given at the time of enrollment.
(7) The school will not assume responsibility for a child who has not been signed in when he/she arrives for the day.

Persons authorized to pick up the child:

_____

_____

_____

  Under no circumstances will the child be released to anyone not known to the school without authorization from parents or guardian.

Persons to be called in case of emergency (be sure to include someone who will usually know your whereabouts):

Name _____ Relationship to child _____

Address _____ Phone _____

Name _____ Relationship to child _____

Address _____ Phone _____

Child's physician _____ Phone _____

Address _____

Emergency hospital preference _____

I hereby give ABC Preschool and Day-Care permission to obtain emergency medical care for _____
                                                   (Child's Name)

Parent's signature _____

Date _____

Figure 91 (continued). Example of a permission form.

_____ whose date of birth is
(Name of Child)

_____ has been enrolled in our school.
Classes meet from two to five times weekly, under the
supervision of a professional teacher and an assistant. The daily
program involves both vigorous and quiet indoor and outdoor
play, including the use of climbing equipment.

Does this child have any physical condition that we should be
aware of? _____

_____

Does this child require special attention, medication, or routine
that may have to be taken into consideration in planning for
his/her time at school? _____

_____

In your opinion, is this child physically and emotionally able to
participate in a day-care program such as the one described
above? _____

_____

Has the child received any of the immunizations listed below?
When?

___ D.P.T. _____   ___ Rubella _____
              (Date)   (Date)

___ Rubeola _____   ___ Polio I _____
                (Date)   (Date)

___ Polio II _____   ___ Polio III _____
                (Date)   (Date)

___ Smallpox _____
                 (Date)

___ Other (specify) _____

Date of last tuberculin test? _____ Result _____

Date of most recent examination _____

We thank you for your help.

_____   _____
(Date)   (Physician's Signature)

Figure 92. *Example of physician's statement.*

ABC Preschool and Day-Care

Week of: _____

Child: _____

Monday
  IN
  _____   _____
        Time   Signature of Parent
  OUT
  _____   _____
        Time   Signature of Parent

Tuesday
  IN
  _____   _____
        Time   Signature of Parent
  OUT
  _____   _____
        Time   Signature of Parent

Wednesday
  IN
  _____   _____
        Time   Signature of Parent
  OUT
  _____   _____
        Time   Signature of Parent

Thursday
  IN
  _____   _____
        Time   Signature of Parent
  OUT
  _____   _____
        Time   Signature of Parent

Friday
  IN
  _____   _____
        Time   Signature of Parent
  OUT
  _____   _____
        Time   Signature of Parent

Figure 93. Example of a daily sign-in sheet.

ABC Preschool and Day-Care
(posted on a bulletin board)

Children are to file orderly out of the building to the opposite side of the parking lot. Teachers are to account for each child. The last staff member out of the room is to close the classroom door. The last staff member out of the building is to close the outside door.

Tornado—Children are to file orderly out of the classroom into the center hall and assume a kneeling position, head on the floor next to the wall, with hands over head.

Other Emergencies—In case of other emergencies (i.e., gas leak, chemical leak, etc.), children will be evacuated and parents will be contacted immediately.

Figure 94. Example of a disaster plan.

```
                ABC Preschool and Day-Care
                (posted on a bulletin board)
                      FIRE DRILLS

Evacuation
   Date         Time of Day      # Children        # Staff
_____    _____   _____    _____


_____                  _____
     (Date)                             (Supervisor's Signature)

                    TORNADO DRILLS

Evacuation
   Date         Time of Day      # Children        # Staff
_____    _____   _____    _____


_____                  _____
     (Date)                             (Supervisor's Signature)
```

Figure 95. *Example of fire and tornado drill form.*

```
                ABC Preschool and Day-Care

Day-care payments of _____ were paid to ABC
                          (Amount)
Preschool and Day-Care for the care of _____
                                            (Child's Name)
from _____ to _____ during the year of 19___.


_____                  _____
     (Date)                             (Supervisor's Signature)
```

Figure 96. *Example of an income tax record for day-care.*

ABC Preschool and Day-Care

Dear Parents,

As happens every year, the chicken pox are once again evident in the community. Being no exception to the rule, we have had cases here at the day-care center. Because our children are together for some time during each day, it is likely that your child has been exposed to chicken pox.

Please watch your child very closely for the following symptoms:

(1) Low-grade fever
(2) Tired or listless feeling
(3) Small red bumps with white blisters

Your child may not have a fever or feel badly, and may have only a few blisters.

The incubation period is fourteen to twenty-nine days. A child may return to school when the last blister scabs.

I ask that you please check your child each morning before coming to the center. This will help us keep further exposure to a minimum.

If you have questions or concerns, please call.

Sincerely,

Director

Figure 97. Example of medical information letter.

Parents need to be kept aware of illnesses that are reported at the day-care center. The purpose is to keep children at home so that the whole school will not be infected. Figures 98 and 99 show forms relating to medication use.

Tuition Increases

Tuition increases must occur periodically in order for the school to keep up with the pace of inflation. This is always a touchy issue, and should be handled tactfully. If possible, mention the possibility of an increase in advance so that parents are prepared when it occurs. Figures 100 and 101 demonstrate

```
┌─────────────────────────────────────────────────────────────┐
│              ABC Preschool and Day-Care                      │
│                                                              │
│      ILLNESS AND MEDICATION PERMISSION SHEET                 │
│                                                              │
│   A child with a fever and other signs of contagion WILL NOT │
│   BE ADMITTED to the day-care center. If such signs develop  │
│   while in our care you will be notified and expected to pick up │
│   your child.                                                │
│   A child on continuing medication with his/her DOCTOR'S     │
│   PERMISSION to return will be administered this medication on │
│   a DAILY BASIS ONLY. This special request form releasing the │
│   center from liability must be signed by the parent daily. No │
│   medication will be given without parental signature. Please try │
│   to make the dosages as near as possible to lunch time      │
│   (11:30–12:30) and/or afternoon snack time (3:00–3:30).     │
│   In making this request I release the day-care from all liability │
│   resulting from the use of this medication.                 │
│                                                              │
│                                                              │
│   ─────────────────        ─────────────────────────        │
│        (Date)                   (Parent's Signature)         │
└─────────────────────────────────────────────────────────────┘
```

Figure 98. Example of a medication permission sheet.

```
┌─────────────────────────────────────────────────────────────┐
│              ABC Preschool and Day-Care                      │
│      (to be attached to medication permission sheet)         │
│                                                              │
│   Child: _____        │
│   Date: _____        │
│   Class: _____        │
│   *Dosage: _____        │
│   Time to be given: _____        │
│   Medicine given at: _____        │
│                                 (Time)                       │
│   Medicine given by: _____        │
│                                (Signature)                   │
│                                                              │
│   *All medicine must be stored in the director's office.     │
└─────────────────────────────────────────────────────────────┘
```

Figure 99. Example of medication chart.

206

how this can be done, while at the same time show how the matter of summer sessions might be addressed.

Program

Children in day-care are going to be in the program for six to nine hours daily, which is a long day for a child. The staff should provide enough stimulating activities to keep the child interested (not entertained). The day-care center *should not* be a baby-sitter, but rather an educator of young children.

The day-care program should be an extended preschool program offering the same early childhood education curricula and activities (refer to Chapter Seven). To provide this extended program, a teacher must plan his/her day with great care. Figure 102 gives an example of how this might be done.

Television

Although there are many good educational programs on television, a quality day-care program does not use the television to keep children busy. Children should be provided with a good early childhood program, not simply entertainment.

Room Environment, Equipment, Play Area

These will be the same as for the preschool, which were discussed in Chapter Five. Figure 103 shows how a preschool facility might be organized, while Figure 104 provides a possible lesson plan.

Naps

COTS

In all day-care programs, cots are probably the most often heard complaint. Cots are expensive, cumbersome, and unsafe.

ABC Preschool and Day-Care

March 18, 1990
Dear Parents,

It is getting close to the end of our school year and is now time to make plans for next year.

Some of the following questions may not apply to your child, but please complete those that do and return to us by March 29th.

Child's Name: _____ Age: _____

SPRING BREAK: (April 8–12)
(1) Will your child be in day-care this week? _____ yes _____ no
(2) Do you need care that week for an older brother or sister?
      _____ yes _____ no If yes, names _____

SUMMER SCHEDULE:
(1) Will your child be attending day-care during the summer?
      _____ yes _____ no
(2) Do you know your vacation dates so we will have an idea of the number of children to expect weekly?
      _____ yes _____ no If yes, dates _____
(3) Do you need care for brothers or sisters? (age three to ten years) _____ yes _____ no If yes, names _____

(4) Of course, our lunch program will be different this summer. Do you have any suggestions as to what we can serve that the children will like? Type of meal, food, etc. _____

FALL SCHEDULE:
(1) Will your child be attending day-care in the fall?
      _____ yes _____ no

Figure 100. Example of letter to parents regarding summer schedule.

(2) If so, do you wish your child enrolled in either Pre-kindergarten or Kindergarten class in the regular preschool program?

(3) Do you have other children you wish to enroll for fall?
Name   Age

_____

_____

I would like your comments on our program. Please be specific and feel free to make criticisms. Remember, we improve the program by your input. It helps us to see your side of our program, and lets us work together for your child.

Comments: _____

_____

_____

_____

As you know we will close the week of June 3rd–7th, July 4th, and the week of August 5th–9th. Please be aware of these dates so you can make other arrangements for your child prior to these times.

Also, because of expenses, we are going to have an increase in tuition beginning with the summer program. We find we must have more income to continue our program, but we will keep the increase to a minimum.

I wish to thank all of you for your understanding and patience this year. We are into the swing of things now and all is going smoothly.

Sincerely,

Director

Comments: _____

_____

_____

_____

Figure 100 (continued). Example of letter to parents regarding summer schedule.

ABC Preschool and Day-Care

April 10, 1990
Dear Parents,

As you know per a previous letter, our rates are going to increase this summer. There are several factors that the school
board must consider in order to keep the day-care center open.
Currently we are operating with a deficit each week. Because
day-care has to be self-supporting, the school board met and
reevaluated our financial situation.

After lengthy consideration, the school board decided the following:

(1) The weekly fee will be raised to $42.50 (including
    lunches).
(2) The $42.50 must be guaranteed, meaning every child will
    owe that amount each week, whether in attendance or not.
(3) The center will be closed for the week between Christmas
    and New Year's, and you will be allowed one (1) week for vaca-
    tion and one (1) week of sick days per year. These three weeks
    are the only weeks for which you will not be charged.

Even though we have reached the above decisions, we now face
the problem of operating during the summer months. As of now,
we only have an enrollment of nineteen children. In order to
cover the operating expenses, we must be filled to capacity
(thirty-three children) at all times. Therefore, if capacity enrollment for the summer is not met, we will be forced to close.

To help decide this matter, we need your answers to the following questions:

(1) Considering the tuition raise and guarantee, will your child
    be enrolled this summer? _____ yes _____ no
(2) Do you know anyone who needs our service for the sum-
    mer? _____ yes _____ no   If so, please give name
    and phone number: _____
(3) If we are forced to close during the summer, will your child
    return to us in the fall? _____ yes _____ no

Figure 101. *Example of a rate increase letter.*

(4) Please write any comments or suggestions.

_____

_____

We will let you know the final decision regarding summer school by May 15th. In order to meet this deadline, please return this letter by May 1, 1990. If we do not receive your response to these questions by May 1, we will assume you are not planning on attending this summer.

Thank you for your understanding and opinions. By working together, hopefully we can resolve these problems.

Sincerely,

Director

Figure 101 (continued). Example of a rate increase letter.

ABC Preschool and Day-Care

Opening: 7:30 A.M.

Preschool classes: 8:00–11:00
(Each teacher will post daily preschool schedule.)

Clean up: 11:00–11:10

Wash for lunch: 11:10–11:30

Lunch: 11:30–12:00

Prepare for nap: 12:00–12:15

Bathroom: 2:45–3:00

Outside play: 3:00–4:00

Indoor play: 4:00–5:25

Closing: 5:30 P.M.

Figure 102. Example of a teacher's daily schedule.

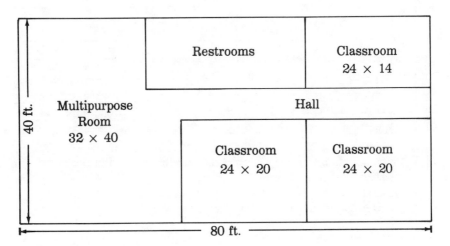

Figure 103. Sample facility diagram—ABC Preschool and Day-Care.

They are very difficult to store and require much storage space. An alternative to cots is to purchase foam mats. These are easier and safer to store. Before purchasing anything for naptime, check state regulations, because they may require a specific item.

PLACEMENT OF CHILDREN AT NAPTIME

All children are required to nap, and most states require that a certain amount of space be left between the children while they are resting. It takes a fairly large room to nap children. However, more than one room can be used. Allow enough space when planning the placement of equipment in the room. In addition every child must have his/her own labeled blanket, sheet, and pillow. These are to be laundered weekly.

Labeling

Every time a child brings or wears an item that will be removed (coat, hat, etc.), it must be labeled with his/her full name.

	MONDAY	TUESDAY	WEDNESDAY	THURSDAY	FRIDAY
8:00–8:35	Opening Calendar Pledge Weather	Opening Calendar Pledge Weather	Opening Calendar Pledge Weather	Opening Calendar Pledge Weather Talk about address	Opening Calendar Pledge Weather Talk about cooperation
8:35–9:00	Activity group Practice cutting	Cutting lines	Trace patterns Cut pieces for rocket	Draw picture of house–address on bottom	Make paper plate bears
9:00–9:45	Learning centers	Learning centers	Learning centers	Learning centers	Learning centers
9:45–10:00	Snack and bathroom	Snack and bathroom	Snack and bathroom	Snack and bathroom	Snack and bathroom
10:00–10:30	Small group activities Math sets	Sort Teddy Bear counters by color sets	Play shape Bingo	Practice writing address	Puppet play
10:30–10:45	Outside play/ Library time	Read Teddy Bear book	Read book about shapes	Story about post office/address	Book about cooperation
10:45–11:00	Closing Evaluate day	Closing Evaluate day	Closing Evaluate day	Closing Evaluate day	Closing Evaluate day

Figure 104. Sample daily lesson plans.

213

Toys

Children should not be allowed to bring their personal toys to school. Instead, encourage children to bring books and records that can be shared. Each record/book should be properly labeled with the child's name.

Final Note

Day-care is the program most needed by parents. Although this is a much desired service, the program carries a great responsibility to deliver extended family care, which should be as much like the home as possible. Love is the major emphasis, and if unconditional love is practiced the program will be one of quality. A baby-sitter takes care of a child's basic needs, but the day-care program must provide for the needs of the "whole child." Love, trust, care, self-esteem, self-worth, and education of the young child must be priorities.

Financial resources are important to running a quality program physically, but love of the child is the most important component of the program. The staff must have high moral values, and they must exhibit and genuinely feel love of children, so be very selective in choosing staff.

Use the preschool curriculum as a guide for the educational program and make sure to include it every day. Day-care is not a baby-sitting service, but is an educational program that provides a safe loving environment for children to enjoy while their parents are working.

Day-care involves a great deal of hard work, but seeing happy, secure children daily makes all the hard work and headaches worth every minute. Good luck, remember—love children above all else!

ABC Preschool – Preschool and Kindergarten Handbook

I MUST CREATE A SYSTEM, OR BE ENSLAVED
BY ANOTHER MAN'S.

—William Blake

CHOOSING A PRESCHOOL EXPERIENCE

ABC Preschool is a part of the (public, church, private) system in (name of state). As such, it can draw on resources, experiences and materials considerably beyond those available to a comparable program. However, this does not insure academic excellence. It is the proper use of resources that leads to this goal. We believe it is the people, more than resources or programs, that are the key. That is why more effort is spent in carefully selecting teachers and assistants for your children than any other task. Each has been selected specifically to fit his/her role in the school. So, you will find teachers from diverse religious backgrounds, geographic backgrounds, etc., on our staff. They share one thing in common—professional excellence. Because of this, they are given considerable freedom to "tailor" your child's experience in order that it might be the best possible. Our uniqueness lies in the priority of academic excellence, and in the means of achieving this priority—through intense emphasis on an outstanding professional faculty operating in as free and creative an environment as possible.

We recognize there are many other paths to a quality preschool experience. Our town is blessed with most of these. Some stress discipline and behavior, some stress Biblical knowledge, some stress individual skill mastery over socialization, some stress accelerated learning of reading, etc. Each of these is of value. So, in choosing a preschool experience, we urge you to examine the various programs available, and see how their respective emphases coincide with your own priorities. Most schools will be more than willing to explain their programs. The better ones will not try to "sell" their own, but will be frank if they feel your priorities can best be met elsewhere.

May your choice be the correct one!

PURPOSE

ABC Preschool is a nonprofit organization whose purpose is to provide a consistently superior educational experience. Its program provides each child with socialization, creative play, art, music, story time, physical activities, and educational learning experiences in accordance with the individual child's age and ability. The programs are further designed to help the child develop habits of observation, questioning, and listening, and an awareness of his/her own feelings and his/her right to express them. The child learns to make free choices, so long as he/she stays within the limits of consideration for people and things. The child is not expected to conform to an arbitrarily imposed norm of behavior. Children are continually challenged in subtle ways to achieve specific learning goals, enabling them to gain increasing meaning from their surrounding world; to develop an awareness of concepts; to interpret sensory experiences; and ultimately to take the prerequisite steps for developing their minds in preparation for reading and performing other academic tasks.

The programs pursued are designed to give the child time to grow, to explore, to experiment, to discover, to play, to love, and above all, time to be a child.

POLICY

ABC Preschool admits students of any religion, race, color, and national or ethnic origin to all the rights, privileges, programs, and activities generally accorded or made available to the students of the school. It does not discriminate on the basis of religion, race, color, national or ethnic origin in administration of its educational policies, admissions policies, or other school-administered programs.

Children must be at least three years old and toilet trained before entering regular preschool classes. A child is enrolled in a class upon receipt of a completed application form and registration fee. Children can be enrolled by telephone. Kindergarten children must be five years old by October 1st to be enrolled, and must have a birth certificate, health examination, and immunization certificate on file at the school.

ACCREDITATION

ABC Preschool is licensed by the State Department of Education, following the standards of the state of (_____). The school is also approved and regularly inspected by the state fire marshall's office.

STAFF

Staff members belong to state and local professional early childhood associations. The director is a member of the Association for Children

Under Six and its state and national affiliates. All staff members are experienced early childhood educators. All are required to keep abreast of professional developments and keep alert to the ever-changing needs of today's families and current research regarding young children.

SCHOOL DATES

ABC Preschool operates on the same schedule as the district of _____ schools. Basically the same vacations and holidays are taken at ABC Preschool as by the local school district. Snow days are also taken with the district schools. (There are snow makeup days provided in our calendar.) Each school year's academic calendar is given at the beginning of the school year during parent orientation meetings. Other holidays may be built into the calender. You will be notified personally concerning these, if needed, although they are exceedingly rare.

TRANSPORTATION AUTHORIZATION

Each child will be assigned a card bearing a letter or number at the beginning of school. This card is to be used by an authorized person in picking him/her up. Children will not be released to anyone without the card, and until written or verbal authorization is presented. This procedure is for your child's safety and will be enforced. Also, for your child's safety, children are always personally escorted to and from vehicles by staff members. It is not the policy of the school to allow children to be "dropped off" by parents, baby-sitters, etc.

CAR POOL

We will help parents find others to form a car pool. Car pooling is tricky and we offer the following suggestions:

- Have your child ready. Take him/her to the car.
- Be home to receive your child.
- Let driver know you are there.
- If child is ill, notify driver ahead of time.
- Include no more than six children in a car pool.
- Check your car for safety.
- Always lock car doors.
- Drive carefully.
- Do not hurry. Life is more precious than time.

Staff members are not permitted to drive children to and from school except in emergency situations.

FINANCIAL

Tuition is based on the actual cost of operating the school. Fees are based on a total year cost for each child, divided into nine equal payments. Payment is due on or before the first day of each month, beginning September 1st. Credit for a prolonged illness or an emergency can be arranged through the director. No credit is given for vacations or holidays.

A registration fee is due when the child is enrolled. A supply fee (determined by class enrolled) is due on or before the September payment. Two consecutive months of delinquent tuition payments will result in automatic withdrawal from the school rolls, unless previous arrangements have been made with the director.

Portraits are taken of each child during the year. However, parents are not required to purchase the picture package.

WHAT TO WEAR, BRING, ETC.

Think of your child's comfort and provide simple, washable, and sturdy clothing. As weather changes, so should clothing. Please provide ample apparel. It is easier to remove an unneeded item than to put on something we don't have. Please label all items brought to school. If your child is prone to accidents, it is a good idea to leave an extra set of clothing at school.

No toys are to be brought to school. Play and toys are already carefully chosen in accordance with the program. Your child may, however, bring a book or record to share with the class at story time. Please put his/her name on these items.

HEALTH

Your child's health is a matter of major importance to all of us. If your child is ill, he/she cannot enjoy the school experience and his/her illness may jeopardize the health of others. We recognize children also may have emotional and physical problems, and the staff is prepared to work in cooperation with you and your professional needs in these areas.

The school asks that you keep your child home:

- if he/she has or has had a fever during the previous twenty-four hour period
- if he/she has a constant cough
- if he/she has vomiting or diarrhea
- if he/she is cranky, fussy, and generally not himself/herself
- if he/she has symptoms of a communicable disease

Please notify us if your child has been exposed to a communicable disease so that we can discuss incubation period when it can be determined which days he/she should stay home. If the school hears of health matters it feels you should be aware of, the school will notify you.

In case of accidental injury, the school will make an immediate and concentrated attempt to contact a parent. If we can't contact you or someone you have specified on your emergency sheet, we will call the child's physician. If necessary, we will call an ambulance or paramedic. Until the arrival of a parent, physician, ambulance, or paramedic, the director or an assistant will be in charge and make all decisions about the care of the child. You will be expected to assume responsibility for any resultant expenses not covered by the school's insurance. The school will maintain a signed parental consent form agreeing to these provisions. It is your responsibility to keep it up-to-date for your child's benefit.

NUTRITION

A snack is served midway through the daily program, usually consisting of juice and cookies. Parents are welcome to send snacks upon approval of the teacher. Birthdays can also be celebrated during snack time. Again, make arrangements with your child's teacher. Occasionally, your child will have the opportunity to cook his/her own snack.

PARENT-TEACHER RELATIONS

Conferences

Two conferences are scheduled for the year, fall and spring. You are welcome to schedule a conference at any other time during the year by contacting your child's teacher. It is important for us to work together in aiding your child's growth.

Parent Group

A parent group meets at scheduled times during the year for programs (lectures by professionals, etc.) of interest to you. These will be announced in advance, so plan to attend. Knowing that others have the same joys, sorrows, and questions you do helps parents to understand themselves and better understand their children.

Programs

Children will present at least two programs during the year—Christmas and Graduation. Individual teachers may put on other programs in addition to these.

Volunteers

Parents will at times be asked to help in classroom activities, accompany us on trips, programs, and other activities. This gives you an opportunity to share in your child's school experience. Of course, visits by parents are always welcome.

Newspaper

Kid Khatter, the school newsletter, is published monthly. It will include a letter from the director giving important information; news from each class; parent or board announcements; and other items of interest. This newsletter is for your information, and it is important that you read it.

Teacher Messages

Messages will be taken by the secretary and relayed to your child's teacher. Teachers cannot be called out of class to answer the phone. Please keep this in mind when planning your call. Emergency messages will be relayed immediately.

TO OUR PARENTS

- We want you to know, to understand, and to discuss with us our programs and goals.
- We want you to feel free to talk to us and ask questions.
- We want you to realize the validity of play as a teaching medium, and the importance of what your child is learning.
- We want to work together with you to help your child develop his/her full potential.

CLASS INFORMATION SHEET

Class Information

Teachers: _____

Supply Fee: _____ Due: September and January

Tuition: _____ Tuition is due by the 1st of each month.

Please make checks payable to: ABC Preschool, and bring to school.

Insurance

Insurance for your child while at school is included in your initial supply fee. Students are covered while participating in activities sponsored and supervised by the policy holder, and while traveling with a group in connection with such activities.

Open House

This time is scheduled for your child to meet the teachers and see his/her classroom. It is not a regular school day. Please remain with your child and limit your stay to ten to fifteen minutes.

Other Charges

A fee of $10.00 will be added to tuition, which is fifteen days past due. A fee of $10.00 will be charged on all returned checks and future payments will be required in cash only.

SCHOOL DATES

The school operates on its own schedule, but taking basically the same Christmas and Spring vacations as the district schools.

Snow and bitter cold days *only* will be taken with the district schools. When county schools are closed because of either of these conditions, we will also be closed. When district schools are on a one hour delay, we will begin classes at the regular time. We are *not* on a one hour delay.

Flu days will be determined by our absentee count—you will be notified by note or telephone if we are closing.

School Calendar

- August 18–22: Orientation
- August 25: School begins
- September 1: Labor Day
- November 27–28: Thanksgiving
- Dec. 19–Jan. 2: Christmas vacation
- January 5: School resumes
- April 6–10: Spring break
- May 20: Last day of school

ARRIVAL AND DISMISSAL

Please pull up to sidewalk, and we will get your child in and out of the car. Please do not leave your car to come to the door. Have your identification card in the window to make loading faster.

It is important to arrive on time—children learn by regularity. It is equally important to pick up your child on time, as teachers have meetings and/or other classes to attend, and will not be responsible for your child after class.

If you are a member of a car pool, please give the director a list of names making up your car pool. If your child is going to ride with someone other than the usual escort, any day, please notify the school. Whoever picks up your child must have the identification card before we will release the child.

Verbal messages relayed to the teacher by a child will not be accepted. Please send all messages by note or talk to your child's teacher. If you have questions or feel disturbed by something your child has told you, please contact your child's teacher to discuss your concern. This helps to keep communication lines open and correct any misunderstandings before they get out of hand.

TRIPS

During the school year, groups will have educational activities. These will be discussed with the children, and parents will be notified by memo before each activity. Blanket permission forms for the school year will be given to you. If you wish your child to participate in these outside activites, this form must be signed and placed on file in the school office.

The hours of these activities will be the same as the school hours and we will be asking parents to help drive. If at all possible, volunteer to go with your child. It means a great deal to the children when their parents take part in school activities.

ABC Preschool and Day-Care– Day-Care Handbook

'TIS EDUCATION FORMS THE COMMON MIND;
JUST AS THE TWIG IS BENT THE TREE'S INCLINED.
—Alexander Pope

_____ , Director

Dear Parents,

We realize that you would prefer to care for your child in your own home, but since you have enrolled your child with us, we shall try to give him/her the loving attention and training that all children need in their early, most formative years.

We welcome your child to our program and we hope this learning experience will be happy and productive. We also invite you to visit us often, ask any questions, or make any suggestions. Only through a good understanding and close working relationship with you can your child benefit fully from this experience. With a clear picture of our day-care program, we trust you will be able to pursue your own work without worry, confident that you have made the best possible arrangements for your child.

PARENT-CHILD ABUSE POLICY

If the center suspects or is aware of any child abuse in the home, such abuse will be reported to the proper authorities immediately. All such reports will be recorded and kept on file. The center will follow any and all requests issued by the proper authorities regarding these matters.

STAFF-CHILD ABUSE POLICY

All staff abuse incidents will be immediately reported to the proper authorities, including the police and a social worker. All reports will constitute grounds for immediate dismissal of the staff member involved.

223

QUESTIONS

If you have any questions regarding the program or the staff, feel free to call or come by any time. We do our best to make your child's stay a happy one while he/she is away from home.

INSURANCE

If you do not have medical and/or surgical insurance for your child, we can provide it at the rate of _____ per year.

LABELS

Upon arrival at the day-care center, all children's personal belongings must be labeled. Also, your child should have a tote bag (with his/her name on it), in which to put his/her personal belongings.

DELINQUENT ACCOUNTS

Accounts must be paid in full each week, or your child will not be admitted on the following Monday. If other financial arrangements are necessary, they must be made with the director.

DISCHARGE PLANS

Parents should discuss discharge plans with the director when a child is to leave permanently. This enables us to prepare the child for leaving and to plan for the future use of his/her place in the group. Two weeks' notice prior to his/her discharge is required. If the center must dismiss a child, the parent will receive written notice.

DISCIPLINE POLICY

Children will be treated in a patient manner while in the center. Children will never be physically disciplined in any manner.

MEDICATION FOR YOUR CHILD

If your child is to take medicine while at day-care, you must sign the medication permission form each day giving permission for him/her to receive medication. A parent must pick up the medicine at the end of the day. Your child will not be allowed to pick it up. Any medicine that is left in the day-care center after 5:30 P.M. on Friday afternoons will be disposed of.

If there is any question regarding the communicability of your child's illness, you may be asked to take him/her home or to give us a written statement from your child's doctor that specifies the child is well enough to return to school. If a child is sick, please keep him/her at home.

DAY-CARE FEES

Hourly:	$2.50	Three full days
Daily:	$10.00	constitutes
Weekly:	$45.00	a full week

A 20% discount does apply for the second child.

PAYMENT OF FEES

Payment is to be made only to the secretary and/or the director on Friday afternoon. If neither one is available you may leave your payment in the payment envelope that is posted on the bulletin board. You may mail us your payment if it is more convenient for you. If you must pay at any time other than Friday afternoon, please make arrangements with the director.

Children who stay with us for short periods only, must pay in advance for their care.

Additional fees will be charged for children remaining in the center after 5:30 P.M., at the rate of $5.00 for each fifteen minutes.

Additional fees will also be charged for any returned checks at the rate of $10.00 per check, and that debit must be paid in cash within twenty-four hours or your child will be refused admittance to the center until such time as you have made other arrangements with the director.

Outstanding balances that are one month old will automatically disqualify your child's admittance. We do not usually send out statements. Therefore, it is your responsibility to see that your account is paid before this deadline.

WHO MAY ATTEND OUR DAY-CARE?

This service is open to all children without regard to gender, race, ethnic background, or religious preference. However, a child must be three years old and toilet trained to be admitted.

HOLIDAYS AND WEEKS THAT DAY-CARE WILL BE CLOSED

The day-care center will be closed:

- Thanksgiving Day
- December 24 through January 1st
- Memorial Day
- First full week of June
- July 4th
- First full week of August
- Labor Day

TELEPHONE MESSAGES

You may telephone from 7:15 A.M.–5:30 P.M., Monday through Friday at 555-5555. Messages will be relayed to your child's teacher.

HEALTH

All children must have a physical examination upon admission to the day-care or kindergarten program.

Medical forms are provided at the time of application. Before admission your child must be immunized against:

(1) Diptheria, whooping cough, tetanus

(2) Polio

(3) Measles

(4) TB skin test

These immunizations are required by the Department of Human Resources, Division of Licensing and Regulations.

We expect you to have these forms filled out and returned to us no later than two weeks after your child has been admitted to the program, preferably before admission. If these forms are delayed for any reason, you must inform the director, and he/she will decide if your child may be admitted. This requirement protects your child and all children attending the program.

RECORDS

We keep records of all attendance, health, identification, and full details regarding contacting you at home or work.

TOYS

We have toys and equipment in the school. Therefore, do not allow children to bring toys from home.

CLOTHING

Washable play clothes are suitable. A change of underwear and socks should be kept in your child's cubby. Each child should bring a sheet and small blanket from home to use at naptime. This blanket and sheet should be taken home each Friday to be laundered and brought back to the center on Monday.

FOOD

The children will be served a morning and an afternoon snack. A wholesome meal will be served at noon, for the price of $1.00 per day. Please be sure that your child has had breakfast and is dressed before coming to school.

The center is licensed by the Department of Human Resources, and inspected and approved by:

(1) County Health Department
(2) County and State Fire Departments

THE FOLLOWING POLICIES ARE IN EFFECT

Hours

We open at 7:30 A.M. and close at 5:30 P.M., Monday through Friday. If you cannot call for your child at the usual time, we expect you to inform us promptly. Remember, your child will be expecting you! Also, if you are going to be detained later than 5:30 P.M., let us know so that we can make the necessary arrangements for one of our staff to remain with your child until you can pick the child up, or make arrangements for someone else to call for your child.

Entrance Procedures

(1) Fill out registration forms and return to ABC Preschool and Day-Care promptly.

(2) The physical examination form must be filled out by your child's doctor and returned to us no later than two weeks following the child's entrance to our program.

(3) Each child must be brought into the building by a parent and picked up by a parent in the afternoon. A sign-in sheet will be on the bulletin board. Parents *must* sign the child in and out each day, stating the exact times of arrival and departure.

(4) *Do not drop your child off at the door—ever!*

(5) A child will not be permitted to leave with anyone other than a parent unless you give us a written note stating that someone else has your permission to call for the child.

(6) In case of emergency, you may telephone us. Do not telephone us or give us verbal instructions for someone else's child.

(7) If you pick up your child other than at checkout time, be sure that the teacher is informed.

(8) A conference will be scheduled for parents with the teacher and the director for problems that cannot be resolved in the center.

DAY-CARE SCHOOL CALENDAR

- August 20–24: Orientation
- August 27: School begins
- September 3: Labor Day
- October 24: Parent-Teacher conference
- November 22, 23: Thanksgiving
- December 24–31: Christmas
- January 1: Vacation
- January 2: School begins
- February 22: Parent-Teacher conference
- April 8–12: Spring break
- May 17: Last day of school

The day-care center will be open and in session on the same days as the county school system. In the event of bad weather, the day-care center will be closed if the county schools are closed.